Antique Glass
Swirl Marbles

Stanley A. Block

Schiffer Publishing Ltd

4880 Lower Valley Road, Atglen, PA 19310 USA

Dedication

This book is dedicated to all marble collectors . . . past, present
and future, in the hope it will enlighten their collecting activities.

Copyright © 2001 by Stanley A. Block
Library of Congress Control Number: 2001092354

Designed by John P. Cheek
Cover design by Bruce M. Waters
Type set in Franklin Gothic No. 2/Garamond
ISBN: 0-7643-1459-9
Printed in China
1 2 3 4

Published by Schiffer Publishing Ltd.
4880 Lower Valley Road
Atglen, PA 19310
Phone: (610) 593-1777; Fax: (610) 593-2002
E-mail: Schifferbk@aol.com
Please visit our web site catalog at
www.schifferbooks.com
We are always looking for people to write books on new
and related subjects. If you have an idea for a book
please contact us at the above address.

This book may be purchased from the publisher.
Include $3.95 for shipping.
Please try your bookstore first.
You may write for a free catalog.

In Europe, Schiffer books are distributed by
Bushwood Books
6 Marksbury Ave.
Kew Gardens
Surrey TW9 4JF England
Phone: 44 (0)20-8392-8585
Fax: 44 (0)20-8392-9876
E-mail: Bushwd@aol.com
Free postage in the UK. Europe: air mail at cost

Marble Collectors Society of America

The Marble Collectors ' Society of America was founded in 1975 as a non-profit organization established for charitable, scientific, literary, and educational purposes. The Society's objectives are to gather and disseminate information and perform services to further the hobby of marbles, marble collecting, and the preservation of the history of marbles and marble making. The Society currently has over 2,000 contributors.

Society projects include the quarterly newsletter, *Marble Mania*, color marble photograph plates, a videotape series, and contributor's listings. In addition, we are in the process of ongoing research, and the development of a collection of marbles for the Society library, which will be available on a loan basis to libraries and museums.

Other major accomplishments of the Society to date are the uninterrupted issuance of a quarterly newsletter, *Marble Mania*; various surveys; photographing and publishing color sheets; gathering and placing collections in museums (The Smithsonian, The Corning Museum of Glass, and the Wheaton Village Museum); publication of price guides, with periodic updates; work toward establishing a library of articles and marble related materials; preparation of slide presentations; preparation and publication of contributor listings; research and issuance of articles concerning marble factories and contemporary marble makers; publication of Mark Randall's booklet, *Marbles as Historical Artifacts*; preparation of videotapes on marbles, including the first two-hour videotape on collecting marbles; classification and appraisal services; as well as the books *Marble Mania*, and Robert Block 's *Marbles: Identification and Price Guide*.

In addition to the above, the Society is working on additional tabletop books covering all facets of the hobby of marbles. These books will expand on the book *Marble Mania* that was published in 1998.

Each book will be a photographic manual, covering a specific section of the hobby. Each book is planned to contain over 500 photographs. The first of these expanded books, *Contemporary Marbles and Related Art Glass,* by Mark Block, was published in October 2000. It contains over 800 photographs representing well over 100 glass artisans.

The next book published was a book on *Sulphide Marbles,* authored by Stanley Block and M. Edwin Payne, published in May 2001. The hardcover book, *Sulphide Marbles,* contains over 600 photographs and is the first of three books covering antique handmade glass marbles. This is the second book, covering the subject of antique handmade glass marbles of the swirl types in detail with more than 850 color photographs.

Acknowledgments

I would like to thank the collectors who have allowed us to view and photograph their collections for inclusion in the Society archives and publications. Our book series would certainly be incomplete without your help and examples.

My sincerest thanks to all who have supported the Marble Collectors Society of America and its efforts to make the hobby of marbles a success. I would also like to thank all that have kept us informed of current events, articles, and other printed materials concerning all facets of the hobby.

I would be remiss if I did not thank my family (Claire, Bob, Mark, and Jonathan) for their help in getting this work into a format usable by our publisher.

We also acknowledge, with our thanks, the assistance and professionalism of Peter Schiffer and his staff at Schiffer Publishing Ltd. Without their capable work our book projects would be delayed.

Thank you all.
Stanley A. Block, chairman
Marble Collectors Society of America

Contents

Introduction

Swirl marbles comprise one of the largest categories of antique handmade glass marbles. There are a number of distinct types that fall into this category.

Swirl marbles are very collectible and are readily available to collectors who seek them. They were produced from the 1800s up to World War I. As far as can be determined, all were produced in Germany and Austria. However, it is believed that immigrant glass workers did produce some in the United States during their off-hours. We can find no proof that this variety of marbles was made commercially in this country.

Very little is known about the history and production of antique marbles. Although efforts continue, there has been very little success in searching out the history of these gems.

Swirl marbles in huge quantities were imported up to World War I. At that time, imports ceased for two reasons: the first being the war, the second being the invention and use of machinery that produced a variety of sizes of glass marbles that were rounder than the imports and much more economical to produce.

Since marbles were the number one toys for boys, their cost and availability were of prime importance. The fact that the rounder marbles were much more accurate in competitive games of the era also helped the takeover of the industry by U.S. manufacturers.

This book is intended to be a photographic manual of antique glass swirl marbles and will show the varieties of swirls, their designs, intricacies, and color variations. It is not intended to be a textbook.

Antique glass swirl marbles are highly sought after collectibles. As such, the collecting public places a great deal of importance on type, size, condition, and eye appeal. We have tried to show as many examples, variations, and color combinations as possible.

Also for the collecting public, price is a factor. Therefore, we have included a summary of average prices for each category shown, with notes for special features. This book is not intended to be a definitive price guide. For comprehensive pricing, we recommend consulting the most recent edition of the society price guide, *Marbles – Identification and Price Guide*, by Robert Block.

Photographs without attribution throughout this book are from the author's collection or Block 's Box L.L.C. archives.

Chapter 1.
Latticinio Core Swirls

Latticinio core swirls are the most common of the handmade glass swirls. Laying colored strands on a glass rod produced them. During production the heated rod with strands is twisted, thereby forming the netting effect. Some examples do not show the netting, as the twist was not tight enough or the strands were too far apart. This type usually appears as sets of strands, see Figures 1-68, 1-109 through 1-111.

Most latticinio cores usually have one or more layers of bands or strands of colored glass close to the surface. It is much more difficult to find "naked" swirls, which are swirls with only the latticinio core. It is even more difficult to find latticinio core swirls in colored glass, see Figures 1-37 through 1-53.

The most common latticinio core color is white, followed by yellow. Next is a combination of alternating white and yellow strands. Harder to find are single color cores of orange, red, green, or blue in that order, with blue being the most difficult (see Figures 1-100 through 1-125).

Alternating strand colors that are harder to find are orange and white, yellow and orange, red and white, green and white, and blue and white, in that order, with blue and white being the hardest to find (see Figures 1-126 through 1-155).

Rarer examples have the core strands placed in a form other than alternating, see Figures 1-98, 1-99, 1-141 through 1-147. Also, the number of design layers affects design and rarity (see Figures 1-28 through 1-36, 1-90 through 1-93).

Occasionally, latticinio marbles have added attractions that increase their rarity. This may include mica chips, aventurine bands, and end of cane marbles with missing design or designs coming through the surface (see Figures 1-58 through 1-67, 1-92 through 1-99, 1-151, 1-152).

Latticinio Swirls

Size	Mint	Near-Mint	Good	Collectible
1/2" to 11/16"	15.00	8.00	5.00	2.00
3/4" to 1"	35.00	20.00	7.00	3.00
1-1/8" to 1-1/2"	125.00	65.00	30.00	20.00
1-5/8" to 1-7/8"	175.00	125.00	60.00	20.00
2" and over	250.00	150.00	75.00	30.00

*All values in dollars

Premiums for:		Examples:
Unusual core colors	1.1 to 10x	1-100 through 1-125
Two or more core colors	1.5 to 10x	1-126 through 1-155
Naked	2 to 5x	1-1
Three-stage	1 to 3x	1-28 through 1-36, 1-90 through 1-93
End-of-cane	3 to 10x	1-54 through 1-67, 1-94 through 1-99
Colored glass	3 to 10x	1-37 through 1-53, 1-60, 1-61
Mica	2 to 5x	1-128
Aventurine in bands	3 to 10x	1-151, 1-152

Deductions for:	
Buffed surface	10 to 20%
Off-center or missing designs	20 to 40%
Ground and polished surface	20%
Annealing or other fractures	25 to 50%

Figure 1-1. Naked white latticinio swirl, 1" d. *Collection of Jerry Biern.*

Figure 1-4. Two stage white latticinio swirl with four outer bands, bluish tint to glass, 1-1/16" d.

Figure 1-2. Two stage white latticinio swirl with three outer bands, 11/16" d.

Figure 1-5. Two stage white latticinio swirl, 1-1/16" d. End view of Figure 1-4.

Figure 1-3. Two stage white latticinio swirl, 11/16" d. End view of 1-2.

Figure 1-6. Two stage white latticinio swirl with unusual outer bands, 1-1/2" d.

Figure 1-7. Two stage white latticinio swirl with four wide outer bands, greenish blue tint to glass, 1-3/4" d.

Figure 1-10. Two stage white latticinio swirl, 11/16" d. End view of Figure 1-9.

Figure 1-8. Two stage white latticinio swirl, 1-3/4" d. End view of Figure 1-7.

Figure 1-11. Two stage white latticinio swirl with four wide alternating bands, 7/8" d.

Figure 1-9. Two stage white latticinio swirl with four thin bands – no twist, 11/16" d.

Figure 1-12. Two stage white latticinio swirl, 7/8" d. End view of Figure 1-11.

Figure 1-13. Two stage white latticinio swirl with four wide outer bands – all with the same colors, 11/16".

Figure 1-16. Two stage white latticinio swirl, 21/32" d. End view of Figure 1-15.

Figure 1-14. Two stage white latticinio swirl, 11/16" d. End view of Figure 1-13.

Figure 1-17. Two stage white latticinio swirl with six outer bands, 21/32" d.

Figure 1-15. Two stage white latticinio swirl with six red outer strands, 21/32" d.

Figure 1-18. Two stage white latticinio swirl, 21/32" d. End view of Figure 1-17.

Figure 1-19. Two stage white latticinio swirl with six outer bands, 1-1/4" d.

Figure 1-20. Two stage white latticinio swirl with four different outer band colors, 1-1/4" d. End view of Figure 1-19.

Figure 1-21. Two stage white latticinio swirl with six outer bands – five different outer band colors, 1-3/4" d.

Figure 1-22. Two stage white latticinio swirl, 1-3/4" d. End view of Figure 1-21.

Figure 1-23. Two stage white latticinio swirl with six alternating color outer bands – perfect proportions, 13/16" d.

Figure 1-24. Two stage white latticinio swirls, 13/16" d. Same cane.

Figure 1-25. Two stage white latticinio swirl with eight outer bands – alternating colors, 1-3/4" d.

Figure 1-28. Three stage white latticinio swirl with three middle blue & white bands. Three outer bands alternating with three yellow strands. 11/16" d.

Figure 1-26. Two stage white latticinio swirl, 1-3/4" d. End view of Figure 1-25.

Figure 1-29. Three stage white latticinio swirl, 11/16" d. End view of Figure 1-28.

Figure 1-27. Two stage white latticinio swirl with double twisted core, 1-7/8" d.

Figure 1-30. Three stage white latticinio swirl with four wide middle bands; six two color outer bands, 1-3/4" d.

Figure 1-31. Three stage white latticinio swirl, 1-3/4" d. End view of Figure 1-30.

Figure 1-34. Three stage white latticinio swirl with four wide middle bands; fifteen yellow outer strands, 1-1/2" d.

Figure 1-32. Three stage white latticinio swirl with four wide middle bands, ten outer strands, 15/16" d.

Figure 1-35. Three stage white latticinio swirl, 1-1/2" d. End view of Figure 1-34.

Figure 1-33. Three stage white latticinio swirl, 15/16" d. End view of Figure 1-32.

Figure 1-36. Three stage white latticinio swirl with eleven yellow alternating with eleven red strands on two levels, 1-3/8" d.

Figure 1-37. Two stage white
latticinio swirl with white core with
eleven outer strands in amethyst
glass, 23/32" d.

Figure 1-40. Two stage white
latticinio swirl, 1-1/4" d. End view
of Figure 1-39.

Figure 1-38. Two stage white
latticinio swirl, 23/32" d. End view
of Figure 1-37.

Figure 1-41. Two stage white latticinio swirl with
six outer bands – blue glass, 1-3/4" d. *Collection of
Elliot Pincus.*

Figure 1-39. Two stage white latticinio
swirl with white core with fourteen
white outer strands in amber glass,
1-1/4" d.

Figure 1-42. Two stage white latticinio swirl
with outer band error – teal blue glass, 7/8"
d. *Collection of Elliot Pincus.*

Figure 1-43. Two stage white latticinio swirl, 7/8" d. End view of Figure 1-42. *Collection of Elliot Pincus.*

Figure 1-46. Two stage white latticinio swirl with blue glass, 1-5/16" d. *Collection of Jerry Biern.*

Figure 1-44. Two stage white latticinio swirl with blue glass, 13/16" d. *Collection of Jerry Biern.*

Figure 1-47. Two stage white latticinio swirl, 1-5/16" d. End view of Figure 1-46. *Collection of Jerry Biern.*

Figure 1-45. Two stage white latticinio swirl, 13/16" d. End view of Figure 1-44. *Collection of Jerry Biern.*

Figure 1-48. Two stage white latticinio swirl with four wide outer bands, 13/16" d.

Figure 1-49. Two stage white latticinio swirl, 13/16" d. End view of Figure 1-48.

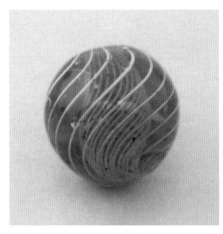

Figure 1-52. Two stage white latticinio swirl with green glass, thirteen outer strands, 7/8" d.

Figure 1-50. Two stage white latticinio swirl with green glass, 13/16" d. *Collection of Jerry Biern.*

Figure 1-53. Two stage white latticinio swirl, 7/8" d. End view of Figure 1-52.

Figure 1-51. Two stage white latticinio swirl, 13/16" d. End view of Figure 1-50. *Collection of Jerry Biern.*

Figure 1-54. Error white latticinio swirl with blue tint to glass – missing one yellow band, 11/16" d.

18

Figure 1-55. Error white latticinio swirl, 11/16" d. End view of Figure 1-54.

Figure 1-58. Error white latticinio swirl, ¾" d. *Collection of Marble Collectors Society.*

Figure 1-56. Error white latticinio swirl, 7/8" d. The design comes through the end of the marble.

Figure 1-59. Error white latticinio swirl with blue glass, 11/16" d. *Collection of Elliot Pincus.*

Figure 1-57. Error white latticinio swirl, 19/32" d.

Figure 1-60. Error white latticinio swirl with amber glass, 11/16" d.

Figure 1-61. Error white latticinio swirl, 11/16" d. End view of Figure 1-60.

Figure 1-64. Error white latticinio swirl, 19/32" d.

Figure 1-62. Error white latticinio swirl with single pontil, end of cane, ¾" d. *Collection of Les Jones.*

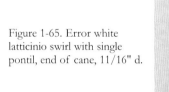

Figure 1-65. Error white latticinio swirl with single pontil, end of cane, 11/16" d.

Figure 1-63. Error white latticinio swirl, 1-3/8" d. Parts of two marbles.

Figure 1-66. Error white latticinio swirl, 11/16" d. End view of Figure 1-65.

Figure 1-67. Error white latticinio swirl with single pontil, 13/16" d. *Collection of Symon Brown.*

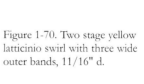

Figure 1-70. Two stage yellow latticinio swirl with three wide outer bands, 11/16" d.

Figure 1-68. Two stage yellow latticinio swirl with three bands close to the core, 11/16" d.

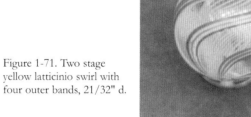

Figure 1-71. Two stage yellow latticinio swirl with four outer bands, 21/32" d.

Figure 1-69. Two stage yellow latticinio swirl, 11/16" d. End view of Figure 1-68.

Figure 1-72. Two stage yellow latticinio swirl with three outer bands, one missing outer band, 13/16" d.

Figure 1-73. Two stage yellow latticinio swirl, 13/16" d. End view of Figure 1-72.

Figure 1-76. Two stage yellow latticinio swirl with six outer bands, 11/16" d.

Figure 1-74. Two stage yellow latticinio swirl with four outer bands, 13/16" d.

Figure 1-77. Two stage yellow latticinio swirl, 11/16" d. End view of Figure 1-76.

Figure 1-75. Two stage yellow latticinio swirl with five outer bands, 21/32" d.

Figure 1-78. Two stage yellow latticinio swirl with six outer bands, bluish tint to glass, 15/16" d.

Figure 1-79. Two stage yellow latticinio swirl, 15/16" d. End view of Figure 1-78.

Figure 1-82. Two stage yellow latticinio swirl with six outer bands, 2" d.

Figure 1-80. Two stage yellow latticinio swirl with six outer bands, bluish tint to glass, 1-1/2" d.

Figure 1-83. Two stage yellow latticinio swirl, 2" d. End view of Figure 1-82.

Figure 1-81. Two stage yellow latticinio swirl, 1-1/2" d. End view of Figure 1-80.

Figure 1-84. Two stage yellow latticinio swirl with six outer bands, 15/16" d.

Figure 1-85. Two stage yellow latticinio swirl, 15/16" d. End view of 1-84.

Figure 1-88. Two stage yellow latticinio swirl, 1-1/4" d. End view of Figure 1-87.

Figure 1-89. Three stage yellow latticinio swirl, 13/16" d. *Collection of Jerry Biern.*

Figure 1-86. Two stage yellow latticinio swirl with eight outer bands, 1-5/8" d.

Figure 1-87. Two stage yellow latticinio swirl with fourteen outer bands, 1-1/4" d.

Figure 1-90. Three stage yellow latticinio swirl, 2" d.

Figure 1-91. Three stage yellow latticinio swirl, 2" d. End view of Figure 1-90.

Figure 1-94. Error yellow latticinio swirl, 5/8" d.

Figure 1-92. Three stage yellow latticinio swirl, 2" d.

Figure 1-95. Error yellow latticinio swirl, 7/8" d. *Collection of Elliot Pincus.*

Figure 1-93. Three stage yellow latticinio swirl, 2" d. End view of Figure 1-92.

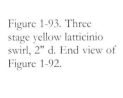

Figure 1-96. Error yellow latticinio swirl, 13/16" d. End of cane.

Figure 1-97. Error yellow latticinio swirl, 13/16" d. End view of Figure 1-96.

Figure 1-100. Orange core latticinio swirl with four outer bands, 11/16" d.

Figure 1-98. Error yellow latticinio swirl with yellow core with one red strand, 13/16" d.

Figure 1-101. Orange core latticinio swirl with four outer bands, 7/8" d.

Figure 1-99. Error yellow latticinio swirl, 13/16" d. End view of Figure 1-98.

Figure 1-102. Orange core latticinio swirl, 7/8" d. End view of Figure 1-101.

Figure 1-103. Orange core latticinio swirl with six outer bands, 1" d.

Figure 1-106. Orange core latticinio swirl, 1" d. End view of Figure 1-105.

Figure 1-104. Orange core latticinio swirl, 1" d. End view of Figure 1-103.

Figure 1-107. Orange core latticinio swirl with six outer bands, 1-5/8" d.

Figure 1-105. Orange core latticinio swirl with six outer bands, 1" d.

Figure 1-108. Orange core latticinio swirl, 1-5/8" d. End view of Figure 1-107.

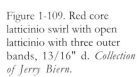

Figure 1-109. Red core latticinio swirl with open latticinio with three outer bands, 13/16" d. *Collection of Jerry Biern.*

Figure 1-112. Red core latticinio swirl with three outer bands, 13/16" d.

Figure 1-110. Red core latticinio swirl, 13/16" d. End view of Figure 1-109. *Collection of Jerry Biern.*

Figure 1-113. Red core latticinio swirl with four outer bands, 13/16" d.

Figure 1-111. Red core latticinio swirl with three outer bands, 13/16" d.

Figure 1-114. Red core latticinio swirl with orange/red core and four outer bands, 21/32" d.

Figure 1-115. Red core latticinio swirl, 21/32" d. End view of Figure 1-114.

Figure 1-118. Red core latticinio swirl, rust red with four outer bands, 1-1/2" d.

Figure 1-116. Red core latticinio swirl, rust red with four outer bands, 1-1/8" d.

Figure 1-119. Red core latticinio swirl, rust red with four outer bands, 1-1/2".

Figure 1-117. Red core latticinio swirl, 1-1/8" d. End view of Figure 1-116.

Figure 1-120. Blue core latticinio swirl, blue latticinio in a blue cage, 1" d. *Collection of Peter Sharrer.*

Figure 1-121. Blue core latticinio swirl, 1" d. End view of Figure 1-120. *Collection of Peter Sharrer.*

Figure 1-124. Green core latticinio swirl, four outer bands, 23/32" d.

Figure 1-122. Blue core latticinio swirl, blue latticinio in a blue cage, 7/8" d. *Collection of Elliot Pincus.*

Figure 1-125. Green core latticinio swirl, 23/32" d. End view of Figure 1-124.

Figure 1-123. Blue core latticinio swirl, baby blue latticinio, ¾' d. *Collection of Elliot Pincus.*

Figure 1-126. Two color core latticinio swirls, 2-5/16" d. Pair of the same cane yellow and white latticinio. *Collection of Bill Sweet.*

Figure 1-127. Two color core latticinio swirls, 2-5/16" d. End view of Figure 1-126. *Collection of Bill Sweet.*

Figure 1-130. Two color core latticinio swirl, four outer bands – greenish tinted glass, 1-5/8" d.

Figure 1-128. Two color core latticinio swirl, alternating yellow and white with mica chips, 2-1/8" d.

Figure 1-131. Two color core latticinio swirl, 1-5/8" d. End view of Figure 1-130.

Figure 1-129. Two color core latticinio swirl, alternating yellow and white with mica chips, 2-1/8" d.

Figure 1-132. Two color core latticinio swirl, six outer bands – alternating yellow and white core, 7/8" d.

Figure 1-133. Two color core latticinio swirl, 7/8" d. End view of Figure 1-132.

Figure 1-137. Two color core latticinio swirl, yellow and white core in blue glass, 11/16" d.

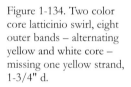

Figure 1-134. Two color core latticinio swirl, eight outer bands – alternating yellow and white core – missing one yellow strand, 1-3/4" d.

Figure 1-138. Two color core latticinio swirl, yellow and white core in blue glass, 5/8" d.

Figure 1-135. Two color core latticinio swirl, 1-3/4" d. End view of Figure 1-134.

Figure 1-139. Two color core latticinio swirl, orange and white core – four outer bands, 9/16" d.

Figure 1-136. Two color core latticinio swirl, yellow and white core, ¾' d. *Collection of Jerry Biern.*

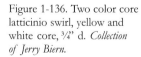

Figure 1-140. Two color core latticinio swirl, 9/16" d. End view of Figure 1-139.

Figure 1-141. Two color core latticinio swirl, orange and yellow core, 1-1/8" d. *Collection of Hansel de Sousa.*

Figure 1-145. Two color core latticinio swirl, red and yellow core with three wide outer bands, 1-1/4" d. *Collection of Jerry Biern.*

Figure 1-142. Two color core latticinio swirl, orange and yellow core, 7/8" d.

Figure 1-146. Two color core latticinio swirl, red and white core – four wide outer bands, 13/16" d.

Figure 1-143. Two color core latticinio swirl, orange and yellow core with six outer bands, 1-3/8" d.

Figure 1-147. Two color core latticinio swirl, 13/16" d. End view of Figure 1-146.

Figure 1-144. Two color core latticinio swirl, 1-3/8" d. End view of Figure 1-143.

Figure 1-148. Two color core latticinio swirl, red and white core – four wide outer bands, 1-1/2" d.

Figure 1-149. Two color core latticinio swirl, red and white core – four wide outer bands, 1-1/2" d.

Figure 1-152. Two color core latticinio swirl, 1-3/4" d. End view of Figure 1-151.

Figure 1-150. Two color core latticinio swirl, 1-1/2" d. End view of Figure 1-149.

Figure 1-153. Two color core latticinio swirl, blue and white core – four outer bands, 1-1/8" d. *Collection of Jerry Biern.*

Figure 1-154. Two color core latticinio swirl, green and white core – four outer bands, ¾" d. *Collection of Jerry Biern.*

Figure 1 151. Two color core latticinio swirl, blue and white core – four outer bands with aventurine, 1-3/4" d.

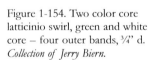

Figure 1-155. Two color core latticinio swirl, ¾" d. End view of Figure 1-154. *Collection of Jerry Biern.*

Chapter 2.
Ribbon Core Swirls

Ribbon core swirls are swirls that have one or two central core bands. Core bands may be thick or thin, wide or narrow, naked or with an outer layer of design.

Single ribbons are slightly more desirable than double ribbons. Rarer are core bands that are very thin (Figure 2-2), double or triple twisted (Figures 2-16, 2-19), or that fills the marble (Figures 2-20, 2-22). Ribbon cores may also include latticinio strands.

Extremely rare is a thin single ribbon in two-color glass. Bands may be opaque or translucent or a combination of both, see Figures 2-14 through 2-17.

Ribbons with mica, aventurine, or translucent colored glasses are rare, as are end-of-cane ribbons.

Ribbon Core Swirls

Size	Mint	Near-Mint	Good	Collectible
1/2" to 11/16"	50.00	30.00	15.00	5.00
3/4" to 1"	80.00	50.00	25.00	10.00
1-1/8" to 1-1/2"	200.00	125.00	75.00	20.00
1-5/8" to 1-7/8"	300.00	200.00	90.00	40.00
2" and over	500.00	350.00	120.00	80.00

*All values in dollars

Premiums for:

		Examples:
Ultra-thin—Wide ribbon	2 to 5x	2-1 through 2-22
Same cane pairs	3x (pair)	2-1, 2-2, 2-54 through 2-56
Three-stage	1 to 3x	2-34 through 2-39, 2-77 through 2-79
End-of-cane	3 to 10x	2-23 through 2-27, 2-67 through 2-76
Colored glass	3 to 10x	2-14 through 2-17

Deductions for:

Double ribbons	20 to 30%
Buffed surface	10 to 20%
Distorted or very thick ribbon	25 to 40%
Off-center or missing designs	20 to 40%
Ground and polished surface	20%
Annealing or other fractures	25 to 50%

Figure 2-1. Ribbon core swirls. Naked Ribbon, pair, same cane, thin ribbons, 13/16" d. *Collection of M. Edwin Payne.*

Figure 2-2. Ribbon core swirls. Naked Ribbon, 13/16" d. End view of Figure 2-1. *Collection of M. Edwin Payne.*

Figure 2-3. Ribbon core swirl. Naked Ribbon, thin ribbon, 11/16" d.

Figure 2-7. Ribbon core swirl. Naked Ribbon, thin ribbon, 1-3/8" d.

Figure 2-4. Ribbon core swirl. Naked Ribbon, 11/16" d. Reverse of Figure 2-3.

Figure 2-8. Ribbon core swirl. Naked Ribbon, thin ribbon, 7/8" d. *Collection of Elliot Pincus.*

Figure 2-5. Ribbon core swirl. Naked Ribbon, thin ribbon edged with translucent turquoise, 13/16" d. *Collection of John S. Fleming.*

Figure 2-9. Ribbon core swirl. Naked Ribbon, thin ribbon, 1-5/8" d. *Collection of Elliot Pincus.*

Figure 2-6. Ribbon core swirl. Naked Ribbon, thin ribbon, 13/16" d.

Figure 2-10. Ribbon core swirl. Naked Ribbon, 1-5/8" d. End view of Figure 2-9. *Collection of Elliot Pincus.*

Figure 2-14. Ribbon core swirl. Naked Ribbon, ½ green glass, ½ clear glass, ¾" d. *Collection of Jerry Biern.*

Figure 2-11. Ribbon core swirl. Naked Ribbon, thin ribbon, 2-1/4" d. *Collection of Bill Sweet.*

Figure 2-15. Ribbon core swirl. Naked Ribbon, ¾" d. End view of Figure 2-14. *Collection of Jerry Biern.*

Figure 2-16. Ribbon core swirl. Naked Ribbon, thin ribbon, double twist – ½ clear, ½ green glass, 11/16" d. *Collection of Elliot Pincus.*

Figure 2-12. Ribbon core swirl. Naked Ribbon, 2-1/4" d. End view of Figure 2-11. *Collection of Bill Sweet.*

Figure 2-13. Ribbon core swirl. Naked Ribbon, thin ribbon, 1-3/4" d. *Collection of Bill Sweet.*

Figure 2-17. Ribbon core swirl. Naked Ribbon, 11/16" d. Top view of Figure 2-16. *Collection of Elliot Pincus.*

Figure 2-18. Ribbon core swirl. Naked Ribbon, latticinio type single ribbon, ¾ " d. *Collection of Jerry Biern.*

Figure 2-22. Ribbon core swirl. Naked Ribbon, 7/8" d. End view of Figure 2-21.

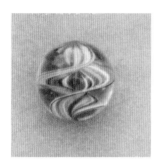

Figure 2-19. Ribbon core swirl. Naked Ribbon, thin triple twist ribbon, ¾" d. *Collection of Elliot Pincus.*

Figure 2-23. Ribbon core swirl. Naked Ribbon, Single Pontil Loop Ribbon, 5/8" d. *Collection of Elliot Pincus.*

Figure 2-20. Ribbon core swirl. Naked Ribbon, ¾" d. End view of Figure 2-19. *Collection of Elliot Pincus.*

Figure 2-24. Ribbon core swirl. Naked Ribbon, 5/8" d. Side view of Figure 2-23. *Collection of Elliot Pincus.*

Figure 2-21. Ribbon core swirl. Naked Ribbon, thin triple twist ribbon, 7/8" d.

Figure 2-25. Ribbon core swirl. Naked Ribbon, 5/8" d. End view of Figure 2-23. *Collection of Elliot Pincus.*

Figure 2-26. Ribbon core swirl. Naked Ribbon, end of cane looped ribbon, ¾" d. *Collection of Bill Sweet.*

Figure 2-30. Two stage ribbon core swirl, ¾" d.

Figure 2-27. Ribbon core swirl. Naked Ribbon, ¾" d. Reverse of Figure 2-26. *Collection of Bill Sweet.*

Figure 2-31. Two stage ribbon core swirl, ¾" d.

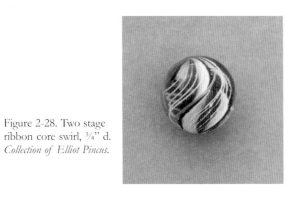

Figure 2-32. Two stage ribbon core swirl. No Twist. 11/16" d.

Figure 2-28. Two stage ribbon core swirl, ¾" d. *Collection of Elliot Pincus.*

Figure 2-29. Two stage ribbon core swirl, ¾" d. *Collection of Elliot Pincus.*

Figure 2-33. Two stage ribbon core swirl, 11/16" d. End view of Figure 2-32.

Figure 2-34. Three stage ribbon core swirl. Single Ribbon. 1-1/4" d.

Figure 2-37. Three stage ribbon core swirl, 2-1/4" d. End view of Figure 2-36. *Collection of John S. Fleming.*

Figure 2-35. Three stage ribbon core swirl, 1-1/4" d. Side view of Figure 2-34.

Figure 2-38. Three stage ribbon core swirl, 23/32" d.

Figure 2-36. Three stage ribbon core swirl, 2-1/4" d. *Collection of John S. Fleming.*

Figure 2-39. Three stage ribbon core swirl, 23/32" d. End view of Figure 2-38.

Figure 2-40. Two stage ribbon core swirl. Latticinio Ribbon – six outer bands. 1-1/2" d.

Figure 2-43. Ribbon core swirl. Naked Double Ribbon, thin, wide ribbon, 11/16" d.

Figure 2-41. Two stage ribbon core swirl, 1-1/2" d. End view of Figure 2-40.

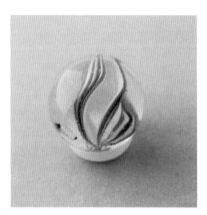

Figure 2-44. Ribbon core swirl. Naked Double Ribbon, 11-16" d. Side view of Figure 2-43.

Figure 2-42. Two stage ribbon core swirl, four outer bands, 7/8" d. *Anonymous.*

Figure 2-45. Ribbon core swirl. Naked Double Ribbon, thin, wide latticinio ribbon, 1-5/8" d.

Figure 2-46. Ribbon core swirl. Naked Double Ribbon, 1-5/8" d. End view of Figure 2-45.

Figure 2-47. Ribbon core swirl. Naked Double Ribbon, thin, wide latticinio ribbon, 2" d. *Collection of Jerry Biern.*

Figure 2-48. Ribbon core swirl. Naked Double Ribbon, 2" d. End view of Figure 2-47. *Collection of Jerry Biern.*

Figure 2-49. Ribbon core swirl. Naked Double Ribbon, two wide bands at side, 5/8" d.

Figure 2-50. Ribbon core swirl. Naked Double Ribbon, two wide bands at side, 1-7/8" d. *Collection of Jerry Biern.*

Figure 2-51. Ribbon core swirl. Naked Double Ribbon, 1-7/8" d. End view of Figure 2-50. *Collection of Jerry Biern.*

Figure 2-52. Ribbon core swirl. Naked Double Ribbon, alternating yellow and white latticinio – two wide outer bands, 1-5/8" d.

Figure 2-53. Ribbon core swirl. Naked Double Ribbon, 1-5/8" d. Second view of Figure 2-52.

Figure 2-57. Two stage Double ribbon core swirls, 21/32" d., 23/32" d. Reverse of Figure 2-56.

Figure 2-54. Two stage Double ribbon core swirls, same cane, two sets of five outer strands, 11/16" d., 23/32" d.

Figure 2-58. Two stage Double ribbon core swirl, ten outer strands, 11/16" d.

Figure 2-55. Two stage Double ribbon core swirls, 11/16" d., 23/32" d. Reverse of Figure 2-54.

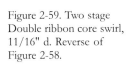

Figure 2-59. Two stage Double ribbon core swirl, 11/16" d. Reverse of Figure 2-58.

Figure 2-56. Two stage Double ribbon core swirls, same cane, sets of outer strands, 21/32" d., 23/32" d.

Figure 2-60. Two stage Double ribbon core swirl, 11/16" d. End view of Figure 2-58.

Figure 2-61. Two stage Double ribbon core swirl, two sets of five outer strands, 1-5/8" d.

Figure 2-64. Two stage Double ribbon core swirl, 1-1/8" d. End view of Figure 2-63.

Figure 2-62. Two stage Double ribbon core swirl, 1-5/8" d. Reverse of Figure 2-61.

Figure 2-65. Two stage Double ribbon core swirl, two sets of five outer strands, English style colors, 1-1/2" d.

Figure 2-63. Two stage Double ribbon core swirl, two eight strand outer bands, 1-1/8" d.

Figure 2-66. Two stage Double ribbon core swirl, 1-1/2" d. End view of Figure 2-65.

Figure 2-67. Two stage Double ribbon core swirl. End of Cane. 5/8" d. *Collection of Hansel de Sousa.*

Figure 2-68. Two stage Double ribbon core swirl, 5/8" d. Top view of Figure 2-67. *Collection of Hansel de Sousa.*

Figure 2-71. Two stage Double ribbon core swirl. Error, end of cane. 7/8" d.

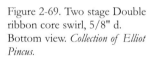

Figure 2-69. Two stage Double ribbon core swirl, 5/8" d. Bottom view. *Collection of Elliot Pincus.*

Figure 2-70. Two stage Double ribbon core swirl, 5/8" d. Top view of Figure 2-69. *Collection of Elliot Pincus.*

Figure 2-72. Two stage Double ribbon core swirl, 7/8" d. Side view of Figure 2-71.

Figure 2-73. Two stage Double ribbon core swirl, 7/8" d. End view of Figure 2-71.

Figure 2-74. Two stage Double ribbon core swirl. Error, end of cane. 19/32" d.

Figure 2-77. Three stage Double ribbon core swirl, second stage – two wide bands. Third stage – two sets of six strands, 1-5/8" d.

Figure 2-75. Two stage Double ribbon core swirl, 19/32" d. End view of Figure 2-74.

Figure 2-78. Three stage Double ribbon core swirl, four outer bands, 21/32" d.

Figure 2-76. Two stage Double ribbon core swirl, 19/32" d. Side view of Figure 2-74.

Figure 2-79. Three stage Double ribbon core swirl, 21/32" d. End view of Figure 2-78.

Chapter 3.
Divided Core Swirls

Divided core swirls are swirls with three or more colored core bands. The core bands can be one color, but are more often a multitude of colors. In addition, each core band may be of different colors. In the case of four core bands, usually two bands of the same colors alternate with two bands of different colors.

There is usually at least one outer layer of design.

Divided cores in translucent colored glass are rare (Figures 3-3, 3-22, and 3-23), as are divided cores with mica or aventurine. More often than not, divided core swirls have an equal number of sets of outer strands or bands as the core bands.

Divided Core Swirls

Size	Mint	Near-Mint	Good	Collectible
1/2" to 11/16"	18.00	10.00	5.00	2.00
3/4" to 1"	45.00	25.00	10.00	5.00
1-1/8" to 1-1/2"	150.00	75.00	40.00	15.00
1-5/8" to 1-7/8"	200.00	110.00	50.00	20.00
2" and over	300.00	200.00	100.00	40.00

*All values in dollars

Premiums for:		Examples:
Five or more core bands	1 to 3x	
Same cane pairs	3x (pair)	3-1
Naked	2 to 5x	3-2, 3-4 through 3-9
Three-stage	1 to 3x	3-42 through 3-47
Four-stage	2 to 5x	3-48, 3-49
End-of-cane	3 to 10x	3-10, 3-24, 3-49, 3-50
Colored glass	3 to 10x	3-3, 3-22, 3-23, 3-40, 3-41

Deductions for:	
Buffed surface	10 to 20%
Off-center or missing designs	20 to 40%
Ground and polished surface	20%
Annealing or other fractures	25 to 50%

Figure 3-1. Naked divided core swirls. Six same cane. Various sizes. *Collection of Jerry Biern.*

Figure 3-2. Naked divided core swirl, three band core, 7/8" d. *Collection of Jerry Biern.*

Figure 3-3. Naked divided core swirl. Three band core – Amber glass. ¾' d. *Collection of Jerry Biern.*

Figure 3-4. Naked divided core swirl, three wide bands, 21/32" d.

Figure 3-5. Naked divided core swirl, four band core, 5/8" d.

Figure 3-6. Naked divided core swirl, four band core, 13/16" d.

Figure 3-7. Naked divided core swirl, 13/16" d. End view of Figure 3-6.

Figure 3-8. Naked divided core swirl, four band core, 1-3/4" d. *Collection of Jerry Biern.*

Figure 3-9. Naked divided core swirl, 1-3/4" d. End view of Figure 3-8. *Collection of Jerry Biern.*

Figure 3-10. Naked divided core swirl, four band core, ¾' d. *Collection of Hansel de Sousa.*

Figure 3-11. Two stage divided core swirl, three band core, 11/16" d. *Collection of Hansel de Sousa.*

Figure 3-12. Two stage divided core swirl, three band core, 7/8" d.

Figure 3-13. Two stage divided core swirl, 7/8" d. End view of Figure 3-12.

Figure 3-17. Two stage divided core swirl, 13/16" d. End view of Figure 3-16.

Figure 3-14. Two stage divided core swirl, three band core, 1-3/16" d.

Figure 3-18. Two stage divided core swirl, three band core, 7/8" d.

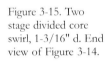

Figure 3-15. Two stage divided core swirl, 1-3/16" d. End view of Figure 3-14.

Figure 3-19. Two stage divided core swirl, 7/8" d. End view of Figure 3-18.

Figure 3-16. Two stage divided core swirl, three band core, 13/16" d.

Figure 3-20. Two stage divided core swirl, three band core, 5/8" d.

Figure 3-21. Two stage divided core swirl, 5/8" d. End view of Figure 3-20.

Figure 3-25. Two stage divided core swirl, four band core, 1" d.

Figure 3-22. Two stage divided core swirl, three band core, green glass, 13/16" d.

Figure 3-26. Two stage divided core swirl, 1" d. End view of Figure 3-25.

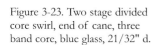

Figure 3-23. Two stage divided core swirl, end of cane, three band core, blue glass, 21/32" d.

Figure 3-27. Two stage divided core swirl, four band core, 1-3/8" d.

Figure 3-24. Two stage divided core swirl, end of cane, three band core, 5/8" d. *Collection of Jeff Yale.*

Figure 3-28. Two stage divided core swirl, four band core, 1" d.

Figure 3-29. Two stage divided core swirl, 1" d. End view of Figure 3-28

Figure 3-33. Two stage divided core swirl, 1" d. End view of Figure 3-32.

Figure 3-30. Two stage divided core swirl, four band core, 7/8" d.

Figure 3-34. Two stage divided core swirl, four band core, 1" d.

Figure 3-31. Two stage divided core swirl, 7/8" d. End view of Figure 3-30.

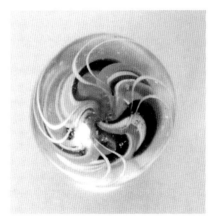

Figure 3-35. Two stage divided core swirl, 1" d. End view of Figure 3-34.

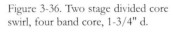

Figure 3-36. Two stage divided core swirl, four band core, 1-3/4" d.

Figure 3-32. Two stage divided core swirl, four band core, 1" d.

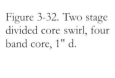

Figure 3-37. Two stage divided core swirl, 1-3/4" d. End view of Figure 3-36.

Figure 3-40. Two stage divided core swirl, four band core, blue glass, 1-7/8" d.

Figure 3-38. Two stage divided core swirl, four band core, 1-5/8" d.

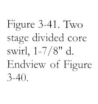

Figure 3-41. Two stage divided core swirl, 1-7/8" d. Endview of Figure 3-40.

Figure 3-39. Two stage divided core swirl, 1-5/8" d. End view of Figure 3-38.

Figure 3-42. Three stage divided core swirl, four band core, 1-5/8" d.

Figure 3-43. Three stage divided core swirl, 1-5/8" d. End view of 3-42.

Figure 3-47. Three stage divided core swirl, 21/32" d. End view of Figure 3-46.

Figure 3-44. Three stage divided core swirl, two layers of three core bands, 21/32" d.

Figure 3-48. Four stage divided core swirl, four band core, 1-1/2" d. *Collection of John S. Fleming.*

Figure 3-45. Three stage divided core swirl, 21/32" d. End view of Figure 3-44.

Figure 3-49. Two stage divided core swirl. End of Cane. 11/16" d.

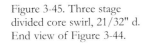

Figure 3-46. Three stage divided core swirl, two layers of three core bands, 21/32" d.

Figure 3-50. Two stage divided core swirl, 11/16" d. End view of Figure 3-49.

Chapter 4
Solid Core Swirls

Solid core swirls have a core of either one solid color or multiple bands of color formed into a solid core. If there are clear spaces between the bands, it is a divided core swirl. If there is only one clear area, it would still be categorized as a solid core.

Solid cores may also be one color with applied strands of color to the core surface. Sometimes these colored strands are a layer above the core. If there is an outer layer of design, it is a triple layer or three stage solid core.

Cores may also be lobed (Figures 4-50 through 4-61). Two, three, and four lobe solid cores are not uncommon, but over four lobes are hard to find. Also, the deeper the troughs in the lobes, the more desirable. The easiest way to identify lobed cores and the number of lobes is to view the marble at the pole.

Naked solid cores (no outside design) (Figures 4-1 through 4-13) are more common than naked latticinio or naked divided core swirls. Translucent solid cores are also hard to find.

Solid core swirls in translucent colored glass or with mica or aventurine are hard to find and therefore are rare.

Solid Core Swirls

Size	Mint	Near-Mint	Good	Collectible
1/2" to 11/16"	20.00	12.00	6.00	3.00
3/4" to 1"	50.00	30.00	20.00	8.00
1-1/8" to 1-1/2"	175.00	125.00	60.00	20.00
1-5/8" to 1-7/8"	225.00	140.00	75.00	20.00
2" and over	300.00	200.00	100.00	40.00

*All values in dollars

Premiums for:		Examples:
Unusual core colors	1.1 to 10x	4-6, 4-13, 4-14, 4-18, 4-26, 4-34, 4-35, 4-40, 4-41
With aventurine	2 to 6x	
Lobed	2 to 5x	4-50 through 4-61
Same cane pairs	3x (pair)	4-14, 4-15, 4-38, 4-39
Naked	2 to 4x	4-1 through 4-13
Three-stage	1 to 3x	4-40 through 4-49
Four-stage	2 to 5x	
End-of-cane	3 to 10x	4-36, 4-37
Colored glass	3 to 10x	4-58, 4-59

Deductions for:	
Buffed surface	10 to 20%
Off-center or missing designs	20 to 40%
Ground and polished surface	20%
Annealing or other fractures	25 to 50%

Figure 4-1. Naked solid core swirl, 1-1/4" d.

Figure 4-5. Naked solid core swirl, 7/8" d. End view of Figure 4-4.

Figure 4-2. Naked solid core swirl, 15/16" d.

Figure 4-6. Naked solid core swirl, translucent purple bands, 7/8" d.

Figure 4-3. Naked solid core swirl, 15/16" d. End view of Figure 4-2.

Figure 4-7. Naked solid core swirl, blue tint to glass, 7/8" d.

Figure 4-4. Naked solid core swirl, 7/8" d.

Figure 4-8. Naked solid core swirl, 7/8" d. End view of Figure 4-7.

Figure 4-9. Naked solid core swirl, 7/8" d.

Figure 4-13. Naked solid core swirl, 1" d. End view of Figure 4-12, one section missing.

Figure 4-10. Naked solid core swirl, 7/8" d. End view of Figure 4-9.

Figure 4-14. Two stage solid core swirls, same cane, 21/32" d.

Figure 4-11. Naked solid core swirl, 1" d.

Figure 4-15. Two stage solid core swirls, 21/32" d. End view of Figure 4-14.

Figure 4-12. Naked solid core swirl, translucent blue and green bands, 1" d.

Figure 4-16. Two stage solid core swirl, 15/16" d.

Figure 4-17. Two stage solid core swirl, 15/16" d. End view of Figure 4-16.

Figure 4-18. Two stage solid core swirl, 13/16" d.

Figure 4-21. Two stage solid core swirl, 1-3/8" d.

Figure 4-22. Two stage solid core swirl, 1" d.

Figure 4-19. Two stage solid core swirl, 1-3/8" d.

Figure 4-23. Two stage solid core swirl, 1" d. End view of Figure 4-22.

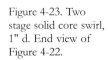

Figure 4-20. Two stage solid core swirl, 1-3/8" d. End view of Figure 4-19.

Figure 4-24. Two stage solid core swirl, 7/8" d.

60

Figure 4-25. Two stage solid core swirl, 7/8" d. End view of Figure 4-24.

Figure 4-29. Two stage solid core swirl, ¾" d.

Figure 4-26. Two stage solid core swirl, 2" d. *Collection of Elliot Pincus.*

Figure 4-30. Two stage solid core swirl, ¾" d. End view of Figure 4-29.

Figure 4-27. Two stage solid core swirl, 7/8" d.

Figure 4-31. Two stage solid core swirl, 1-7/16" d.

Figure 4-28. Two stage solid core swirl, 7/8" d. End view of Figure 4-27.

Figure 4-32. Two stage solid core swirl, 1-7/16" d. End view of Figure 4-31.

Figure 4-33. Two stage solid core swirl, missing one blue core band, 1-1/2" d.

Figure 4-38. Three stage solid core swirls, same cane, 1-1/2" d. *Collection of Jerry Biern.*

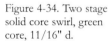

Figure 4-34. Two stage solid core swirl, green core, 11/16" d.

Figure 4-39. Three stage solid core swirls, 1-1/2" d. End view of Figure 4-38. *Collection of Jerry Biern.*

Figure 4-35. Two stage solid core swirl, blue core, 11/16" d.

Figure 4-40. Three stage solid core swirl, translucent green core, 13/16" d.

Figure 4-36. Two stage solid core swirl, end of cane, 5/8" d. *Collection of Richard Lightner.*

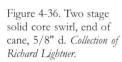

Figure 4-37. Two stage solid core swirl, end of cane, ¾' d. *Collection of Elliot Pincus.*

Figure 4-41. Three stage solid core swirl, 13/16" d. End view of Figure 4-40.

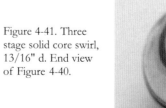

Figure 4-42. Three stage solid core swirl, 7/8" d.

Figure 4-46. Three stage solid core swirl, 1-3/4" d. *Collection of Bernie Benavidez.*

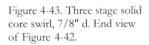
Figure 4-43. Three stage solid core swirl, 7/8" d. End view of Figure 4-42.

Figure 4-47. Three stage solid core swirl, 1-3/4" d. End view of Figure 4-46. *Collection of Bernie Benavidez.*

Figure 4-44. Three stage solid core swirl, 1-5/8" d. *Collection of Jerry Biern.*

Figure 4-48. Three stage solid core swirl, 7/8" d.

Figure 4-45. Three stage solid core swirl, 1-5/8" d. End view of Figure 4-44. *Collection of Jerry Biern.*

Figure 4-49. Three stage solid core swirl, 7/8" d. End view of Figure 4-48.

Figure 4-50. Two stage, three lobed solid core swirl, 13/16" d.

Figure 4-53. Two stage, three lobed solid core swirl, 1-1/4" d.

Figure 4-51. Two stage, three lobed solid core swirl, 13/16" d. End view of Figure 4-50.

Figure 4-54. Two stage, three lobed solid core swirl, 1-1/4" d. End view of Figure 4-53.

Figure 4-52. Two staged, four lobed solid core swirl, 11/16" d.

Figure 4-55. Two stage, three lobed solid core swirl, 15/16" d. *Collection of Jerry Biern.*

Figure 4-56. Two stage, three lobed solid core swirl, 21/32" d.

Figure 4-59. Two stage, three lobed solid core swirl, 23/32" d. End view of Figure 4-58.

Figure 4-57. Two stage, three lobed solid core swirl, 21/32" d. End view of Figure 4-56.

Figure 4-60. Three stage, three lobed solid core swirl, 15/16" d.

Figure 4-58. Two stage, three lobed solid core swirl, green tint to glass, 23/32" d.

Figure 4-61. Three stage, three lobed solid core swirl, 15/16" d. End view of Figure 4-60.

Chapter 5.
Banded (Coreless) Swirls

Banded swirls may have clear or colored glass, or they may be translucent, semi-opaque, or opaque. All have one or more bands or strands applied to, or just below, the outer surface. Some of the rarer ones have vivid base colors with colorful bands. With a loose interpretation some Lutz types, clambroths, peppermints, Indians, gooseberry, Joseph's Coat, custard, and cornhusk marbles could all fall into this category. However, since those latter types have their own more easily recognized categories, they each deserve their own section.

Banded Swirls

Size	Mint	Near-Mint	Good	Collectible
1/2" to 11/16"	25.00	15.00	8.00	4.00
3/4" to 1"	60.00	40.00	15.00	8.00
1-1/8" to 1-1/2"	150.00	80.00	25.00	15.00

*All values in dollars. Above prices are for clear glass banded swirls

Premiums for:		Examples:
Unusual bright color bands	1.5 to 4x	5-51, 5-52, 5-55 through 5-58, 5-76, 5-77
Surface color coverage over 50%	2 to 5x	5-24, 5-25, 5-34, 5-35, 5-55, 5-56
Banded opaque–White base color	5 to 10x	5-22 through 5-49, 5-86 through 5-89
Banded opaque–Colored base color	8 to 20x	5-50 through 5-85
End-of-cane	3 to 5x	5-15 through 5-20, 5-40 through 5-47, 5-57 through 5-60
Colored glass	3 to 5x	5-4 through 5-6, 5-13

Deductions for:	
Buffed surface	10 to 20%
Off-center or missing designs	20 to 40%
Ground and polished surface	20%
Annealing or other fractures	25 to 50%

Figure 5-2. Clear banded swirl, 5/8" d.

Figure 5-3. Clear banded swirl, 11/16" d.

Figure 5-1. Group of transparent clear banded swirls. Various sizes.

Figure 5-4. Clear banded swirl, colored glass, 11/16" d.

Figure 5-9. Clear banded swirl, 13/16" d.

Figure 5-5. Clear banded swirl, colored glass, 11/16" d.

Figure 5-10. Clear banded swirl, 13/16" d. End view of Figure 5-9.

Figure 5-6. Clear banded swirl, colored glass, 11/16" d.

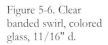

Figure 5-11. Clear banded swirl, 1-1/2" d. *Collection of Jeff Yale.*

Figure 5-7. Clear banded swirl, tinted glass, 11/16" d.

Figure 5-8. Clear banded swirl, tinted glass, 11/16" d.

Figure 5-12. Clear banded swirl, 1-1/2" d. End view of Figure 5-11. *Collection of Jeff Yale.*

Figure 5-13. Clear banded swirl, colored glass, 5/8" d. *Collection of Jerry Biern.*

Figure 5-17. Clear banded swirl, ¾" d. End view of Figure 5-16.

Figure 5-14. Clear banded swirls, colored glass, 5/8" d. to 11/16" d. *Collection of Mike Harrod.*

Figure 5-18. Clear banded swirls, colored glass cane.

Figure 5-15. Clear banded swirl, end of cane, error in design, 11/16" d.

Figure 5-19. Clear banded swirls, colored glass cane.

Figure 5-16. Clear banded swirl, end of cane, single pontil, ¾" d.

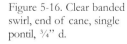

Figure 5-20. Clear banded swirl, error, 9/16" d.

Figure 5-21. Group of Opaque Banded Swirls. Various sizes.

Figure 5-22. Opaque banded swirl, white base, 13/16" d.

Figure 5-24. Opaque banded swirl, white base, 21/32" d.

Figure 5-26. Opaque banded swirl, white base, 21/32" d.

Figure 5-23. Opaque banded swirl, 13/16" d. End view of Figure 5-22.

Figure 5-25. Opaque banded swirl, 21/32" d. End view of Figure 5-24.

Figure 5-27. Opaque banded swirl, 21/32" d. End view of Figure 5-26.

Figure 5-28. Opaque banded swirl, white base, 21/32" d.

Figure 5-32. Opaque banded swirl, white base, 19/32" d.

Figure 5-29. Opaque banded swirl, 21/32" d. End view of Figure 5-28.

Figure 5-33. Opaque banded swirl, 19/32" d. End view of Figure 5-32.

Figure 5-30. Opaque banded swirl, white base, 5/8" d.

Figure 5-34. Opaque banded swirl, white base, 11/16" d.

Figure 5-31. Opaque banded swirl, 5/8" d. End view of Figure 5-30.

Figure 5-35. Opaque banded swirl, 11/16" d. End view of Figure 5-34.

Figure 5-36. Opaque banded swirl, white base, 21/32" d.

Figure 5-40. Opaque banded swirl, white base, single pontil end of cane, 11/16" d.

Figure 5-37. Opaque banded swirl, 21/32" d. End view of Figure 5-36.

Figure 5-41. Opaque banded swirl, 11/16" d. End view of Figure 5-40.

Figure 5-38. Opaque banded swirl, white base, 21/32" d.

Figure 5-42. Opaque banded swirl, white base, single pontil, red, 11/16" d.

Figure 5-39. Opaque banded swirl, 21/32" d. End view of Figure 5-38.

Figure 5-43. Opaque banded swirl, 11/16" d. End view of Figure 5-42.

Figure 5-44. Opaque banded swirl, white base, single pontil, orange, 11/16" d.

Figure 5-48. Opaque banded swirl, white base, four bands, ¾" d. *Collection of Bill Sweet.*

Figure 5-45. Opaque banded swirl, 11/16" d. End view of Figure 5-44.

Figure 5-49. Opaque banded swirl, ¾" d. End view of Figure 5-48. *Collection of Bill Sweet.*

Figure 5-46. Opaque banded swirl, white base, single pontil, green, 11/16" d.

Figure 5-50. Opaque banded swirl, gray base, 11/16" d.

Figure 5-47. Opaque banded swirl, 11/16" d. End view of Figure 5-46.

Figure 5-51. Opaque banded swirl, gray base, 7/8" d. *Collection of Wayne Sanders.*

Figure 5-52. Opaque banded swirl, 7/8" d. End view of Figure 5-51. *Collection of Wayne Sanders.*

Figure 5-56. Opaque banded swirl, 11/16" d. End view of Figure 5-55.

Figure 5-53. Opaque banded swirl, yellow base, 21/32" d.

Figure 5-57. Opaque banded swirl, yellow base, 11/16" d.

Figure 5-54. Opaque banded swirl, 21/32" d. End view of Figure 5-53.

Figure 5-58. Opaque banded swirl, 11/16" d. End view of Figure 5-57.

Figure 5-55. Opaque banded swirl, yellow base, 11/16" d.

Figure 5-59. Opaque banded swirl, end of cane, yellow base, 11/16" d. *Collection of Bill Sweet.*

Figure 5-60. Opaque banded swirl, 11/16" d. End view of Figure 5-59. *Collection of Bill Sweet.*

Figure 5-64. Opaque banded swirl, 21/32" d. End view of Figure 5-63.

Figure 5-61. Opaque banded swirl, green base color, 11/16" d.

Figure 5-65. Opaque banded swirl, green base color, 11/16" d.

Figure 5-62. Opaque banded swirl, 11/16" d. End view of Figure 5-61.

Figure 5-66. Opaque banded swirl, 11/16" d. End view of Figure 5-65.

Figure 5-63. Opaque banded swirl, green base color, 21/32" d.

Figure 5-67. Opaque banded swirl, green base color, 11/16" d.

Figure 5-68. Opaque banded swirl, 11/16" d. End view of Figure 5-67.

Figure 5-72. Opaque banded swirl, blue base color, 9/16" d.

Figure 5-69. Opaque banded swirl, green base color, single pontil, 5/8" d. *Collection of Hansel de Sousa.*

Figure 5-73. Opaque banded swirl, 9/16" d. End view of Figure 5-72.

Figure 5-70. Opaque banded swirl, blue base color, 11/16" d.

Figure 5-74. Opaque banded swirl, blue base color, 11/16" d.

Figure 5-71. Opaque banded swirl, 11/16" d. End view of Figure 5-70.

Figure 5-75. Opaque banded swirl, 11/16" d. End view of Figure 5-74.

Figure 5-79. Opaque banded swirl, 11/16" d. End view of Figure 5-78. *Collection of Bill Sweet.*

Figure 5-76. Opaque banded swirl, blue base color, 11/16" d.

Figure 5-80. Semi Opaque banded swirl, yellow base color, 5/8" d.

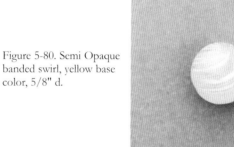

Figure 5-77. Opaque banded swirl, 11/16" d. End view of Figure 5-76.

Figure 5-81. Semi Opaque banded swirl, mauve base color, 7/8" d.

Figure 5-78. Opaque banded swirl, blue base color, 11/16" d. *Collection of Bill Sweet.*

Figure 5-82. Semi Opaque banded swirl, 7/8" d. End view of Figure 5-81.

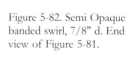

Figure 5-83. Semi Opaque banded swirl, pink base color, 23/32" d.

Figure 5-87. Semi Opaque banded swirl, 7/8" d. End view of Figure 5-86.

Figure 5-84. Semi Opaque banded swirl, 23/32" d. End view of Figure 5-83.

Figure 5-88. Semi Opaque banded swirl, white base color, 19/32" d.

Figure 5-85. Semi Opaque banded swirl, blue base color, 11/16" d.

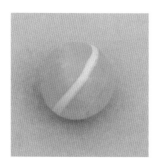

Figure 5-86. Semi Opaque banded swirl, white base color, 7/8" d.

Figure 5-89. Semi Opaque banded swirl, 19/32" d. End view of Figure 5-88.

This is one of the most stunning and desirable categories of swirl marbles. Lutz swirls fall into a number of subtypes. All are highly prized by collectors and are diligently sought out. The various Lutz types include clear and colored glass banded Lutz swirls, semi-opaque and opaque banded Lutz swirls, ribbon Lutz swirls, Indian Lutz, and end of day Lutz.

All of the Lutz types are self explanatory, but to clarify and explain some distinctions regarding the latter types, we offer the following.

Ribbon Lutz may be in clear glass or colored glass, all are transparent. The clear glass ribbons may be of one color or may have one color on each side. The ribbons in colored glass are usually white, but appear to show up as the color of the outer glass.

Indian Lutz swirls are among the most difficult of the Lutz types to find. They usually consist of two or three Lutz bands, with each band edged on both sides with strands of color.

If a bright light can be seen through any of the opaque Lutz's (banded or Indian), they are known as 'maglite' Lutz's.

Very rare items are coffin boxes and sets of Lutz marbles on game boards, see Figures 6-2, 6-42, 6-118.

Lutz Swirls

Size	Mint	Near-Mint	Good	Collectible
1/2" to 11/16"	125.00	80.00	40.00	20.00
3/4" to 1"	175.00	125.00	60.00	30.00
1-1/8" to 1-1/2"	350.00	250.00	125.00	50.00
1-5/8" to 1-7/8"	800.00	500.00	200.00	50.00
2" and over	1,000.00	600.00	300.00	75.00

*All values in dollars. Above prices are for banded clear Lutz swirls

Premiums for:		Examples:
Banded		
Colored glass	2 to 4x	6-24 through 6-45
Semi-opaque glass	2 to 8x	6-46 through 6-66
Opaque and opaque maglites	3 to 5x	6-67 through 6-95
Two different colored bands	5 to 8x	6-3, 6-4
Three sets of bands	3 to 8x	6-70, 6-71, 6-78, 6-79, 6-86 through 6-89
Ribbons		
Clear glass	2 to 4x	6-96 through 6-117
Colored glass	3 to 6x	6-119 through 6-130
Unusual cores	3 to 10x	6-146, 6-147
Rare color combinations	3 to 10x	6-38, 6-39, 6-57, 6-58, 6-65, 6-66, 6-94, 6-95
Indian	5 to 10x	6-131 through 6-139
Same cane pairs	3x (pair)	6-3 through 6-5

Deductions for:		
Buffed surface	10 to 20%	
Off-center or missing designs	20 to 40%	
Ground and polished surface	20%	
Annealing or other fractures	25 to 50%	

Figure 6-1. Clear and colored transparent banded lutz swirls. Various sizes.

Figure 6-2. Group of clear and colored transparent banded lutz swirls. Peewees.

Figure 6-3. Clear banded lutz swirls. Matched pair with two different bands on each. 1-3/16" d. *Collection of M. Edwin Payne.*

Figure 6-4. Clear banded lutz swirls, 1-3/16" d. End view of Figure 6-3. *Collection of M. Edwin Payne.*

Figure 6-5. Clear banded lutz swirls, set of three, same cane, 1-3/16" d. *Collection of M. Edwin Payne.*

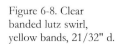
Figure 6-8. Clear banded lutz swirl, yellow bands, 21/32" d.

Figure 6-9. Clear banded lutz swirl, 21/32" d. End view of Figure 6-8.

Figure 6-6. Clear banded lutz swirl, blue tinted glass, 13/16" d.

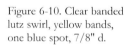
Figure 6-10. Clear banded lutz swirl, yellow bands, one blue spot, 7/8" d.

Figure 6-7. Clear banded lutz swirl, 13/16" d. End view of Figure 6-6.

Figure 6-11. Clear banded lutz swirl, 7/8" d. End view of Figure 6-10.

Figure 6-12. Clear banded lutz swirl, purple bands, 7/8" d.

Figure 6-15. Clear banded lutz swirl, olive green bands, 7/8" d.

Figure 6-13. Clear banded lutz swirl, 7/8" d. End view of Figure 6-12.

Figure 6-16. Clear banded lutz swirl, red bands, 7/8" d.

Figure 6-14. Clear banded lutz swirl, dark purple bands, 13/16" d.

Figure 6-17. Clear banded lutz swirl, 7/8" d. End view of Figure 6-16.

Figure 6-18. Clear banded lutz swirl, orange bands, ¾" d.

Figure 6-21. Clear banded lutz swirl, 7/8" d. End view of Figure 6-20.

Figure 6-19. Clear banded lutz swirl, ¾" d. End view of Figure 6-18.

Figure 6-22. Clear banded lutz swirl, dark blue bands, 15/16" d.

Figure 6-20. Clear banded lutz swirl, light blue bands, 7/8" d.

Figure 6-23. Clear banded lutz swirl, 15/16" d. End view of Figure 6-22.

Figure 6-24. Clear banded lutz swirl, white bands, olive brown tint, 15/16" d.

Figure 6-28. Clear banded lutz swirl, blue bands, amber tint, 7/8" d.

Figure 6-25. Clear banded lutz swirl, 15/16" d. End view of Figure 6-24.

Figure 6-29. Clear banded lutz swirl, 7/8" d. End view of Figure 6-28.

Figure 6-26. Clear banded lutz swirl, yellow bands, amber tint, 7/8" d.

Figure 6-30. Clear banded lutz swirl, red bands, amber tint, 7/8" d.

Figure 6-27. Clear banded lutz swirl, 7/8" d. End view of Figure 6-26.

Figure 6-31. Clear banded lutz swirl, 7/8" d. End view of Figure 6-30.

Figure 6-32. Clear banded lutz swirl, white bands, green tint, 11/16" d.

Figure 6-36. Clear banded lutz swirl, blue bands, green tint, 9/16" d.

Figure 6-33. Clear banded lutz swirl, 11/16" d. End view of Figure 6-32.

Figure 6-37. Clear banded lutz swirl, 9/16" d. End view of Figure 6-36.

Figure 6-34. Clear banded lutz swirl, yellow bands, green tint, 7/8" d.

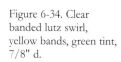

Figure 6-38. Clear banded lutz swirl, orange bands, green tint, ¾" d.

Figure 6-35. Clear banded lutz swirl, 7/8" d. End view of Figure 6-34.

Figure 6-39. Clear banded lutz swirl, ¾" d. End view of Figure 6-38.

Figure 6-40. Clear banded
lutz swirl, white bands, blue
glass, 13/16" d.

Figure 6-44. Clear banded lutz swirl,
blue bands, blue tint, 21/32" d.

Figure 6-41. Clear banded
lutz swirl, 13/16" d. End
view of Figure 6-40.

Figure 6-45. Clear banded lutz swirl,
21/32" d. End view of Figure 6-44.

Figure 6-42. Clear banded
lutz swirl, white bands, blue
tint, 7/8" d.

Figure 6-43. Clear banded
lutz swirl, 7/8" d. End
view of Figure 6-42.

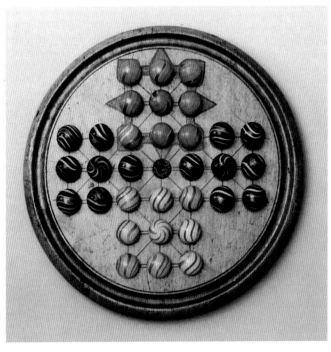

Figure 6-46. Semi Opaque Banded Lutz Swirls. Various sizes.

Figure 6-47. Semi Opaque Banded Lutz Swirl,
white base, red/orange bands, 13/16" d.

Figure 6-50. Semi Opaque Banded Lutz Swirl,
¾" d. End view of Figure 6-49.

Figure 6-48. Semi Opaque Banded Lutz Swirl,
13/16" d. End view of Figure 6-47.

Figure 6-51. Semi Opaque Banded Lutz Swirl,
blue bands, white base, ¾' d.

Figure 6-49. Semi Opaque Banded Lutz Swirl,
white base, red bands, ¾' d.

Figure 6-52. Semi Opaque Banded Lutz Swirl,
¾" d. End view of Figure 6-51.

Figure 6-53. Semi Opaque Banded Lutz Swirl, blue bands, custard base, ¾" d.

Figure 6-56. Semi Opaque Banded Lutz Swirl, 13/16" d. End view of Figure 6-55.

Figure 6-54. Semi Opaque Banded Lutz Swirl, ¾" d. End view of 6-53.

Figure 6-57. Semi Opaque Banded Lutz Swirl, blue bands, purple base, ¾" d.

Figure 6-55. Semi Opaque Banded Lutz Swirl, red bands, custard base, 13/16" d.

Figure 6-58. Semi Opaque Banded Lutz Swirl, ¾" d. End view of Figure 6-57.

Figure 6-59. Semi Opaque Banded Lutz Swirl, blue bands, green base, 19/32" d.

Figure 6-63. Semi Opaque Banded Lutz Swirl, yellow bands, blue base, 9/16" d.

Figure 6-60. Semi Opaque Banded Lutz Swirl, 19/32" d. End view of Figure 6-59.

Figure 6-64. Semi Opaque Banded Lutz Swirl, 9/16" d. End view of Figure 6-63.

Figure 6-61. Semi Opaque Banded Lutz Swirl, yellow bands, lime green base, 13/16" d.

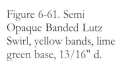

Figure 6-65. Semi Opaque Banded Lutz Swirl, red bands, blue base, ¾" d.

Figure 6-62. Semi Opaque Banded Lutz Swirl, 13/16" d. End view of Figure 6-61.

Figure 6-66. Semi Opaque Banded Lutz Swirl, ¾" d. End view of Figure 6-65.

Figure 6-67. Banded Opaque
Lutz Swirl, white bands with
design error, 21/32" d.

Figure 6-70. Banded
Opaque Lutz Swirl, three
bands of lutz, three white
strands, 21/32" d.

Figure 6-68. Banded
Opaque Lutz Swirl,
21/32" d. Reverse
of Figure 6-67.

Figure 6-71. Banded
Opaque Lutz Swirl, 21/32"
d. End view of Figure 6-70.

Figure 6-69. Banded Opaque
Lutz Swirl, 21/32" d. End
view of Figure 6-67.

Figure 6-72. Banded
Opaque Lutz Swirl, gray
bands, 13/16" d.

Figure 6-73. Banded Opaque Lutz Swirl, 13/16" d. End view of Figure 6-72.

Figure 6-76. Banded Opaque Lutz Swirl, green bands, normal configuration, 11/16" d.

Figure 6-74. Banded Opaque Lutz Swirl, yellow bands, normal configuration, 7/8" d.

Figure 6-77. Banded Opaque Lutz Swirl, 11/16" d. End view of Figure 6-76.

Figure 6-75. Banded Opaque Lutz Swirl, 7/8" d. End view of Figure 6-74.

Figure 6-78. Banded Opaque Lutz Swirl, green bands, 3/3 configuration, 5/8" d.

Figure 6-79. Banded
Opaque Lutz Swirl, 5/8" d.
End view of Figure 6-78.

Figure 6-82. Banded
Opaque Lutz Swirl,
orange/red bands,
normal configura-
tion, 13/16" d.

Figure 6-80. Banded
Opaque Lutz Swirl, red
bands, normal
configuration, 9/16" d.

Figure 6-83. Banded
Opaque Lutz Swirl,
13/16" d. End view
of Figure 6-82.

Figure 6-81. Banded Opaque
Lutz Swirl, 9/16" d. End
view of Figure 6-80.

Figure 6-84. Banded
Opaque Lutz Swirl, blue
bands, normal
configuration, 7/8" d.

Figure 6-85. Banded Opaque Lutz Swirl, 7/8" d. End view of Figure 6-84.

Figure 6-88. Banded Opaque Lutz Swirl, blue bands, lutz out of one band, 3/3 configuration, 21/32" d.

Figure 6-86. Banded Opaque Lutz Swirl, blue bands, 3/3 configuration (3 bands of lutz alternating with 3 colored strands), 11/16" d.

Figure 6-89. Banded Opaque Lutz Swirl, 21/32" d. End view of Figure 6-88.

Figure 6-87. Banded Opaque Lutz Swirl, 11/16" d. End view of Figure 6-86.

Figure 6-90. Banded Opaque Lutz Swirl, blue bands, custard base, 11/16" d.

Figure 6-91. Banded
Opaque Lutz Swirl,
11/16" d. End view
of Figure 6-90.

Figure 6-94. Banded Opaque Lutz Swirl, red
bands, blue base, 7/8" d.

Figure 6-92. Banded Opaque
Lutz Swirl, white bands, blue
base, 13/16" d.

Figure 6-95. Banded Opaque Lutz Swirl, 7/8"
d. End view of Figure 6-94.

Figure 6-93. Banded
Opaque Lutz Swirl,
13/16" d. End view
of Figure 6-92.

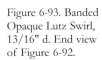

Figure 6-96. Ribbon lutz swirl, translucent red
ribbon, 13/16" d.

Figure 6-97. Ribbon lutz swirl, 13/16" d. End view of Figure 6-96.

Figure 6-100. Ribbon lutz swirl, white opaque ribbon, 7/8" d.

Figure 6-98. Ribbon lutz swirl, translucent orange ribbon, 11/16" d.

Figure 6-101. Ribbon lutz swirl, 7/8" d. End view of Figure 6-100.

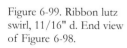 Figure 6-99. Ribbon lutz swirl, 11/16" d. End view of Figure 6-98.

Figure 6-102. Ribbon lutz swirl, white opaque ribbon, blue tinted glass, 13/16" d.

Figure 6-103. Ribbon lutz swirl, 13/16"
d. End view of Figure 6-102.

Figure 6-106. Ribbon lutz swirl, red on white
ribbon, 1-1/4" d.

Figure 6-104. Ribbon lutz swirl, opaque
yellow ribbon, 11/16" d.

Figure 6-107. Ribbon lutz swirl, 1-1/4" d.
End view of Figure 6-106.

Figure 6-105. Ribbon lutz swirl, 11/16"
d. End view of Figure 6-104.

Figure 6-108. Ribbon lutz swirl, yellow and
light purple ribbon, 7/8" d.

Figure 6-109. Ribbon lutz swirl, 7/8" d. End view of Figure 6-108.

Figure 6-112. Ribbon lutz swirl, yellow and blue ribbon, 7/8" d.

Figure 6-110. Ribbon lutz swirl, yellow and light blue ribbon, 13/16" d.

Figure 6-113. Ribbon lutz swirl, 7/8" d. End view of Figure 6-112.

Figure 6-111. Ribbon lutz swirl, 13/16" d. End view of Figure 6-110.

Figure 6-114. Ribbon lutz swirl, red and blue ribbon, ¾" d.

Figure 6-115. Ribbon lutz swirl, ¾" d. End view of Figure 6-114.

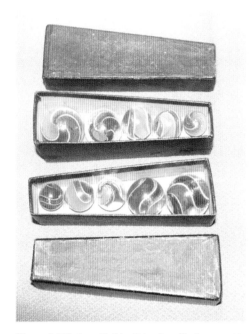

Figure 6-118. Lutz Swirls. Pair of coffin boxes with Ribbon Lutz's. Various sizes. *Collection of Greg Stake.*

Figure 6-116. Ribbon lutz swirl, red and green ribbon, 21/32" d.

Figure 6-119. Ribbon lutz swirl, white ribbon, amber glass, ¾" d.

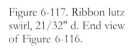

Figure 6-117. Ribbon lutz swirl, 21/32" d. End view of Figure 6-116.

Figure 6-120. Ribbon lutz swirl, ¾" d. End view of Figure 6-119.

Figure 6-121. Ribbon lutz swirl, white ribbon in green glass, 13/16" d.

Figure 6-124. Ribbon lutz swirl, ¾" d. End view of Figure 6-123.

Figure 6-122. Ribbon lutz swirl, 13/16" d. End view of Figure 6-121.

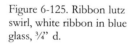 Figure 6-125. Ribbon lutz swirl, white ribbon in blue glass, ¾" d.

 Figure 6-126. Ribbon lutz swirl, ¾" d. End view of Figure 6-125.

Figure 6-123. Ribbon lutz swirl, white ribbon in blue glass, ¾" d.

Figure 6-127. Ribbon lutz swirl, white ribbon in dark blue glass, 11/16" d.

Figure 6-128. Ribbon lutz swirl, 11/16" d. End view of Figure 6-127.

Figure 6-131. Indian lutz swirl, matched pair of three band Indians, 11/16" d.

Figure 6-132. Indian lutz swirl, three bands, each with different band colors, 5/8" d.

Figure 6-129. Ribbon lutz swirl, white ribbon in slate blue glass, 7/8" d.

Figure 6-133. Indian lutz swirl, 5/8" d. End view of Figure 6-132.

Figure 6-130. Ribbon lutz swirl, 7/8" d. End view of Figure 6-129.

Figure 6-134. Indian lutz swirl, three wide lutz bands, 11/16" d.

Figure 6-135. Indian lutz swirl, 11/16" d. End view of Figure 6-138.

Figure 6-139. Indian lutz swirl, 23/32" d. End view of Figure 6-138.

Figure 6-136. Indian lutz swirl, two wide lutz bands, 21/32" d.

Figure 6-140. End of Day Lutz. 11/16" d.

Figure 6-137. Indian lutz swirl, 21/32" d. End view of Figure 6-136.

Figure 6-138. Indian lutz swirl, three wide bands edging the lutz bands, 23/32" d.

Figure 6-141. End of Day Lutz, green glass, 1-7/16" d. *Collection of Bill Tite.*

Figure 6-142. End of Day Lutz. 1-7/16" d. End view of Figure 6-141. *Collection of Bill Tite.*

Figure 6-145. End of Day Lutz, 1-3/8" d. End view of Figure 6-144. *Collection of Bill Tite.*

Figure 6-143. End of Day Lutz. 1-3/8" d.

Figure 6-146. Solid Core Lutz Swirl, core has bands of lutz, 11/16" d.

Figure 6-144. End of Day Lutz. Cloud type. 1-3/8" d. *Collection of Bill Tite.*

Figure 6-147. Solid Core Lutz Swirl, 11/16" d. End view of 6-146.

Clambroths have an opaque or semi-opaque base color with applied surface strands of one or more colors. Clambroth glass is usually an off white. Since some colored glass marbles have the same surface design, they are called black or blue base clams. These usually have one surface strand color, although there are some with two colors, see Figures 7-17 through 7-22.

There is also a clambroth category called cased clams. A cased clam is a normal looking clambroth that has an overlay of clear glass. Also falling into this category are clear glass marbles with a near surface design imitating the clambroth: usually, red or orange bands with white in between (see Figures 7-7 through 7-14).

Clambroths

Size	Mint	Near-Mint	Good	Collectible
1/2" to 11/16"	200.00	100.00	40.00	20.00
3/4" to 1"	300.00	200.00	60.00	30.00
1-1/8" to 1-1/2"	600.00	350.00	100.00	50.00
1-5/8" to 2"	2,000.00	1,200.00	400.00	200.00

*All values in dollars.

Premiums for: | | **Examples:**
| | |
Unusual base colors | 2 to 10x | 7-17 through 7-25
Two or more core colors | 1.5 to 10x | 7-26 through 7-53
Cased | 2 to 5x | 7-7 through 7-14
Rare band design | 2 to 5x | 7-34, 7-35, 7-50 through 7-53

Deductions for:
Buffed surface | 10 to 20%
Off-center or missing designs | 20 to 40%
Ground and polished surface | 20%
Annealing or other fractures | 25 to 50%

Figure 7-1. Clambroth Swirls. Group photo. Various Sizes.

Figure 7-2. Clambroth Swirl. One Color
Bands. Eleven Blue Bands on White.
11/16" d.

Figure 7-5. Clambroth Swirl. One Color
Bands. Purple bands on white. 13/16" d.

Figure 7-3. Clambroth Swirl. One
Color Bands, 11/16" d. End view of
Figure 7-2.

Figure 7-6. Clambroth Swirl. One Color
Bands, 13/16" d. End view of Figure 7-5.

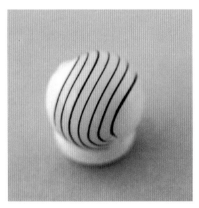

Figure 7-4. Clambroth Swirl. One Color
Bands. Purple bands on white. Missing
most of the bands. 9/16" d.

Figure 7-7. Clambroth Swirl. One Color
Bands. Green bands on white. 11/16" d.

Figure 7-8. Clambroth Swirl. One Color Bands, 11/16" d. End view of Figure 7-7.

Figure 7-11. Clambroth Swirl. One Color Bands. Red bands on white, cased glass, ¾" d.

Figure 7-9. Clambroth Swirl. One Color Bands. Red bands on white, cased glass, 11/16" d. *Collection of Bill Sweet*.

Figure 7-12. Clambroth Swirl. One Color Bands, ¾" d. End view of Figure 7-11.

Figure 7-10. Clambroth Swirl. One Color Bands, 11/16" d. End view of Figure 7-9. *Collection of Bill Sweet*.

Figure 7-13. Clambroth Swirl. One Color Bands. Red bands on white, cased glass, 23/32" d.

Figure 7-14. Clambroth Swirl. One Color Bands, 23/32" d. End view of Figure 7-13.

Figure 7-17. Clambroth Swirl. One Color Bands. White bands on a black base, 13/16" d.

Figure 7-15. Clambroth Swirl. One Color Bands. Red bands on white, 13/16" d.

Figure 7-18. Clambroth Swirl. One Color Bands, 13/16" d. End view of 7-17.

Figure 7-16. Clambroth Swirl. One Color Bands, 13/16" d. End view of Figure 7-15.

Figure 7-19. Clambroth Swirl. One Color Bands. Red bands on a black base, 3/4' d. *Collection of Bill Sweet.*

Figure 7-20. Clambroth Swirl. One Color Bands, ¾" d. End view of Figure 7-19. *Collection of Bill Sweet.*

Figure 7-23. Clambroth Swirl. One Color Bands. White bands on a light blue base, 11/16" d.

Figure 7-21. Clambroth Swirl. One Color Bands. Orange/red bands on a black base, 11/16" d.

Figure 7-24. Clambroth Swirl. One Color Bands, 11/16" d. End view of Figure 7-23.

Figure 7-22. Clambroth Swirl. One Color Bands, 11/16" d. End view of Figure 7-21.

Figure 7-25. Clambroth Swirl. One Color Bands. White bands on a navy blue base, 1-3/4" d.

Figure 7-26. Clambroth Swirl. Two Color Bands. Red alternating with blue on a white base, 13/16" d.

Figure 7-30. Clambroth Swirl. Two Color Bands. Purple alternating with red on a white base, 9/16" d. *Collection of Peter Sharrer.*

Figure 7-27. Clambroth Swirl. Two Color Bands, 13/16" d. End view of Figure 7-26.

Figure 7-31. Clambroth Swirl. Two Color Bands. Purple alternating with red on a white base, 9/16" d. *Collection of Peter Sharrer.*

Figure 7-28. Clambroth Swirl. Two Color Bands. Yellow alternating with black on a white base, 9/16" d.

Figure 7-32. Clambroth Swirl. Two Color Bands. Blue and green on a white base, 21/32" d.

Figure 7-29. Clambroth Swirl. Two Color Bands, 9/16" d. End view of Figure 7-28.

Figure 7-33. Clambroth Swirl. Two Color Bands, 21/32" d. End view of Figure 7-32.

Figure 7-34. Clambroth Swirl. Two Color Bands. Seven blue and five green bands on a white base, ½" d.

Figure 7-37. Clambroth Swirl. Two Color Bands, ¾' d. End view of Figure 7-36.

Figure 7-35. Clambroth Swirl. Two Color Bands, ½' d. End view of Figure 7-34.

Figure 7-38. Clambroth Swirl. Two Color Bands. Red alternating with green bands on a white base, 21/32" d.

Figure 7-36. Clambroth Swirl. Two Color Bands. Green alternating with blue bands on a white base, ¾' d.

Figure 7-39. Clambroth Swirl. Two Color Bands, 21/32" d. End view of Figure 7-38.

Figure 7-40. Clambroth Swirl. Two Color Bands. Red alternating with green on a white base, ¾' d.

Figure 7-41. Clambroth Swirl. Two Color Bands, ¾" d. End view of Figure 7-40.

Figure 7-44. Clambroth Swirl. Multicolor Bands. Red, green, and blue bands on a white base, 13/16" d.

Figure 7-42. Clambroth Swirl. Multicolor Bands. Red, green, and blue bands on a white base, 7/8" d.

Figure 7-45. Clambroth Swirl. Multicolor Bands, 13/16" d. End view of Figure 7-44.

Figure 7-43. Clambroth Swirl. Multicolor Bands, 7/8" d. End view of Figure 7-42.

Figure 7-46. Clambroth Swirl. Multicolor Bands. Purple, green, blue, and red bands on a white base, ¾" d.

Figure 7-47. Clambroth Swirl. Multicolor Bands, ¾" d. End view of Figure 7-46.

Figure 7-50. Clambroth Swirl. Multicolor Bands. Purple, green, and blue bands on a white base, 11/16" d.

Figure 7-48. Clambroth Swirl. Multicolor Bands. Green, red, and blue on a white base; error- missing bands, 13/16" d.

Figure 7-51. Clambroth Swirl. Multicolor Bands, 11/16" d. End view of Figure 7-50.

Figure 7-52. Clambroth Swirl. Multicolor Bands. Blue, green, brown, yellow, and pink bands on a white base, 21/32" d. *Collection of Peter Sharrer.*

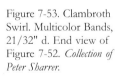

Figure 7-49. Clambroth Swirl. Multicolor Bands, 13/16" d. End view of Figure 7-48.

Figure 7-53. Clambroth Swirl. Multicolor Bands, 21/32" d. End view of Figure 7-52. *Collection of Peter Sharrer.*

Peppermint swirls are marbles that look like peppermint candy. They are red, white, and blue with the colors alternating around the marble and being close to the surface.

The most common type has two wider bands of blue alternating with white and sets of red strands. The number of red and white bands can vary in this type of peppermints, see Figures 8-1 through 8-20.

Another type has two red alternating with two blue bands of about the same size, with wider white sections in between each band. See Figures 8-25 through 8-34. An additional variation has attached red and blue bands alternating with white. These are much harder to find, see Figures 8-21 through 8-24.

The rarest of the peppermints is the first (most common) category adorned with mica chips. See Figures 8-16 through 8-20.

All of the peppermints have the designs close to the surface of the marble. Some collectors confuse this category with ribbon swirls, which have the same colors on the ribbon.

Peppermint Swirls

Size	Mint	Near-Mint	Good	Collectible
1/2" to 11/16"	100.00	60.00	30.00	20.00
3/4" to 1"	200.00	100.00	60.00	30.00
1-1/8" to 1-1/2"	1,000.00	500.00	100.00	50.00
1-5/8" to 1-7/8"	2,500.00	1,250.00	300.00	50.00

*All values in dollars.

Premiums for:		Examples:
Beachball type	2 to 5x	8-25 through 8-34
Unusual colors	2 to 10x	8-33, 8-34
With mica	3 to 10x	8-16 through 8-20
Unusual band design	3 to 5x	8-21 through 8-24

Deductions for:	
Buffed surface	10 to 20%
Off-center or missing designs	20 to 40%
Ground and polished surface	20%
Annealing or other fractures	25 to 50%

Figure 8-1. Peppermint Swirls. Various sizes.

Figure 8-2. Peppermint Swirl. Two Red Bands, normal peppermint, 9/16" d.

Figure 8-6. Peppermint Swirl. Three Red Bands, normal peppermint, ¾" d.

Figure 8-3. Peppermint Swirl. Two Red Bands, 9/16" d. End view of Figure 8-2.

Figure 8-7. Peppermint Swirl. Three Red Bands, ¾" d. End view of Figure 8-6.

Figure 8-4. Peppermint Swirl. Two Red Bands, normal peppermint, 21/32" d.

Figure 8-8. Peppermint Swirl. Three Red Bands, normal peppermint, ¾' d.

Figure 8-5. Peppermint Swirl. Two Red Bands, 21/32" d. End view of Figure 8-4.

Figure 8-9. Peppermint Swirl. Three Red Bands, ¾' d. End view of Figure 8-8.

Figure 8-10. Peppermint Swirl. Three Red Bands, rare size, 1-1/16" d.

Figure 8-11. Peppermint Swirl. Three Red Bands, 1-1/16" d. End view of Figure 8-10.

Figure 8-12. Peppermint Swirl. Three Red Bands, rare size, 1-5/8" d. *Collection of Jerry Biern.*

Figure 8-13. Peppermint Swirl. Three Red Bands, 1-5/8" d. End view of Figure 8-12. *Collection of Jerry Biern.*

Figure 8-14. Peppermint Swirl. Three Red Bands, wide red bands—missing one band on one side, 13/16" d.

Figure 8-15. Peppermint Swirl. Three Red Bands, 13/16" d. End view of Figure 8-14.

Figure 8-16. Peppermint Swirls. Peppermint with Mica. Various sizes.

Figure 8-19. Peppermint Swirl. Peppermint with Mica. Three red bands, rare size, 1-1/2" d.

Figure 8-17. Peppermint Swirl. Peppermint with Mica. Two red bands, 13/16" d.

Figure 8-20. Peppermint Swirl. Peppermint with Mica, 1-1/2" d. End view of Figure 8-19.

Figure 8-21. Peppermint Swirl. Peppermint, alternating bands of red, blue, and white, 21/32" d.

Figure 8-18. Peppermint Swirl. Peppermint with Mica, 13/16" d. End view of Figure 8-17.

Figure 8-22. Peppermint Swirl. Peppermint, 21/32" d. End view of Figure 8-21.

Figure 8-23. Peppermint Swirl. Peppermint, alternating bands of red, blue, and white, 23/32" d.

Figure 8-26. Peppermint Swirl. Peppermint, 21/32" d. End view of Figure 8-25.

Figure 8-24. Peppermint Swirl. Peppermint, 23/32" d. End view of Figure 8-23.

Figure 8-27. Peppermint Swirl. Peppermint, alternating bands of red, blue, and white, 13/16" d.

Figure 8-25. Peppermint Swirl. Peppermint, alternating bands of red, blue, and white, 21/32" d.

Figure 8-28. Peppermint Swirl. Peppermint, 13/16" d. End view of Figure 8-27.

Figure 8-29. Peppermint Swirl. Peppermint, alternating bands of red, blue, and white, 5/8" d.

Figure 8-32. Peppermint Swirl. Peppermint, 19/32" d. End view of Figure 8-31.

Figure 8-30. Peppermint Swirl. Peppermint, 5/8" d. End view of Figure 8-29.

Figure 8-33. Peppermint Swirl. Peppermint, alternating wide bands of orange, blue, and white, 11/16" d.

Figure 8-31. Peppermint Swirl. Peppermint, alternating bands of red, blue, and white, 19/32" d.

Figure 8-34. Peppermint Swirl. Peppermint, 11/16" d. End view of Figure 8-33.

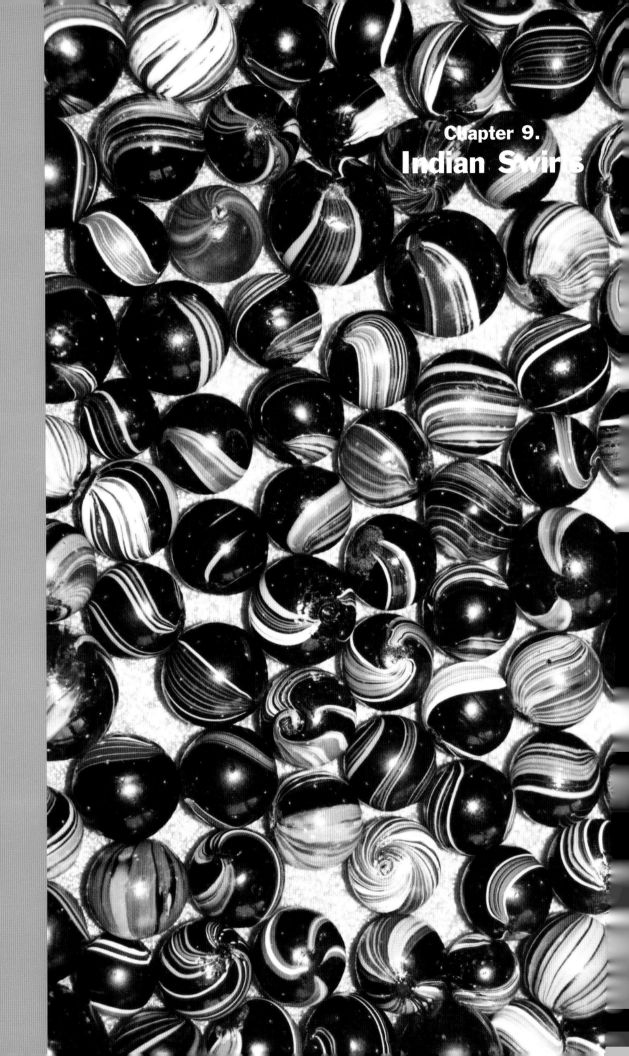

Chapter 9.
Indian Swirls

Indian swirls are usually opaque black or opaque purple base glass with applied bands of color on the surface. The surface bands may be distinct bands (usually two or three) or may be multi-strand sets of color that may cover from 10% to 100% of the surface of the marble. Another variety may have only one or two thin white strands.

In addition to the above opaque and semi-opaque slag glass type Indians, there are also glass marbles that appear to be Indian swirls. However, when a strong light is shown, they are translucent glass. Translucent base glass colors are amber, amethyst, red, blue, and green. If a light shows through the glass, they are known as "maglite" Indians.

Indian Swirls

Size	Mint	Near-Mint	Good	Collectible
1/2" to 11/16"	90.00	50.00	25.00	15.00
3/4" to 1"	125.00	75.00	40.00	15.00
1-1/8" to 1-1/2"	400.00	300.00	125.00	50.00
1-5/8" to 1-7/8"	Too rare to value			
2" and over	Too rare to value			

*All values in dollars. Above prices are for Indian swirls with bands of color

Premiums for:		Examples:
Maglite	1.25x	9-69 through 9-93
Unusual surface colors	1.1 to 10x	9-24 through 9-27
Color coverage of 50 to 75%	1.5 to 3x	9-28 through 9-43
Color coverage of 75 to 100%	3 to 6x	9-44 through 9-68
Same cane pairs	3 to 6x (pair)	9-1 through 9-3
End-of-cane	3 to 10x	9-68 through 9-70

Deductions for:	
Buffed surface	10 to 20%
Off-center or missing designs	20 to 40%
Ground and polished surface	20%
Annealing or other fractures	25 to 50%

Figure 9-1. Indian Swirls. Banded, two band—pair from same cane, 29/32" d. *Collection of Ron & Dee Hetzner.*

Figure 9-2. Indian Swirls. Banded, 29/32" d. Reverse side of Figure 9-1. *Collection of Ron & Dee Hetzner.*

Figure 9-3. Indian Swirls. Banded, 29/32" d. End view of Figure 9-1. *Collection of Ron & Dee Hetzner.*

Figure 9-6. Indian Swirl. Banded, two bands, 11/16" d.

Figure 9-4. Indian Swirl. Banded, two bands—rare size, 1-3/4" d. *Collection of Jerry Biern.*

Figure 9-7. Indian Swirl. Banded, 11/16" d. End view of Figure 9-6.

Figure 9-5. Indian Swirl. Banded, two bands, 11/16" d.

Figure 9-8. Indian Swirl. Banded, two bands, 21/32" d.

Figure 9-9. Indian Swirl. Banded, 21/32" d.
End view of Figure 9-8.

Figure 9-12. Indian Swirl. Banded, two bands,
15/16" d.

Figure 9-10. Indian Swirl. Banded, two bands,
11/16" d.

Figure 9-13. Indian Swirl. Banded, 15/16" d. End
view of Figure 9-12.

Figure 9-11. Indian Swirl. Banded, 11/16" d.
End view of Figure 9-10.

Figure 9-14. Indian Swirl. Banded, two bands,
11/16" d.

Figure 9-15. Indian
Swirl. Banded, 11/16"
d. End view of Figure
9-14.

Figure 9-18. Indian
Swirl. Banded, three
bands, 29/32" d.

Figure 9-16. Indian
Swirl. Banded, two
bands, 13/16" d.

Figure 9-19. Indian
Swirl. Banded, 29/32"
d. End view of Figure
9-18.

Figure 9-17. Indian
Swirl. Banded, 13/16"
d. End view of Figure
9-16.

Figure 9-20. Indian
Swirl. Banded, three
bands, 11/16" d.

Figure 9-21. Indian Swirl. Banded, 11/16" d. End view of 9-20.

Figure 9-24. Indian Swirl. Banded, four bands, 11/16" d.

Figure 9-22. Indian Swirl. Banded, four bands, 21/32" d.

Figure 9-25. Indian Swirl. Banded, 11/16" d. End view of Figure 9-24.

Figure 9-23. Indian Swirl. Banded, 21/32" d. End view of Figure 9-22.

Figure 9-26. Indian Swirl. Banded, six bands, 11/16" d. *Collection of Peter Sharrer.*

Figure 9-27. Indian Swirl. Banded, 11/16" d. End view of Figure 9-26. *Collection of Peter Sharrer.*

Figure 9-31. Indian Swirl. 50-75% Color, 7/8" d. End view of Figure 9-30.

Figure 9-28. Indian Swirl. 50-75% Color, two wide bands, 29/32" d.

Figure 9-32. Indian Swirl. 50-75% Color, 21/32" d.

Figure 9-29. Indian Swirl. 50-75% Color, 29/32" d. End view of Figure 9-28.

Figure 9-33. Indian Swirl. 50-75% Color, 21/32" d. End view of Figure 9-32.

Figure 9-30. Indian Swirl. 50-75% Color, two wide bands, 7/8" d.

Figure 9-34. Indian Swirl. 50-75% Color, 11/16" d.

Figure 9-35. Indian Swirl. 50-75% Color, 11/16" d. End view of Figure 9-34.

Figure 9-38. Indian Swirl. 50-75% Color, ¾" d.

Figure 9-36. Indian Swirl. 50-75% Color, 13/16" d.

Figure 9-39. Indian Swirl. 50-75% Color, ¾" d. End view of 9-38.

Figure 9-37. Indian Swirl. 50-75% Color, 13/16" d. End view of Figure 9-36.

Figure 9-40. Indian Swirl. 50-75% Color, 11/16" d.

Figure 9-41. Indian Swirl. 50-75% Color, 11/16" d. End view of Figure 9-40.

Figure 9-42. Indian Swirl. 50-75% Color, 21/32" d.

Figure 9-43. Indian Swirl. 50-75% Color, 21/32" d. End view of 9-42.

Figure 9-44. Indian Swirl. 360° Color, ¾" d. *Collection of Bill Sweet.*

Figure 9-45. Indian Swirl. 360° Color, ¾" d. End view of Figure 9-44. *Collection of Bill Sweet.*

Figure 9-46. Indian Swirl. 360° Color, 13/16" d. *Collection of Becky Huber.*

Figure 9-47. Indian Swirl. 360° Color, 13/16" d. *Collection of Becky Huber.*

Figure 9-50. Indian Swirl. 360° Color, rare size, 2" d. *Collection of Jerry Biern.*

Figure 9-48. Indian Swirl. 360° Color, rare size, 1-1/2" d. *Collection of Bill Tite.*

Figure 9-51. Indian Swirl. 360° Color, 2" d. End view of Figure 9-50. *Collection of Jerry Biern.*

Figure 9-49. Indian Swirl. 360° Color, rare size, 1-5/8" d. *Collection of Wayne Sanders.*

Figure 9-52. Indian Swirl. 360° Color, 21/32" d.

Figure 9-53. Indian Swirl.
360° Color, 21/32" d. End
view of Figure 9-52.

Figure 9-56. Indian
Swirl. 90% Color,
11/16" d.

Figure 9-54. Indian
Swirl. 80% Color,
11/16" d.

Figure 9-57. Indian
Swirl. 90% Color,
11/16" d. End view
of Figure 9-56.

Figure 9-55. Indian
Swirl. 80% Color,
11/16" d. End view
of Figure 9-54.

Figure 9-58. Indian
Swirl. 80% Color,
11/16" d.

Figure 9-59. Indian Swirl. 80% Color, 11/16" d. End view of Figure 9-58.

Figure 9-62. Indian Swirl. 80% Color, 11/16" d. End view of Figure 9-60.

Figure 9-60. Indian Swirl. 80% Color, 11/16" d.

Figure 9-63. Indian Swirl. 80% Color, 13/16" d.

Figure 9-61. Indian Swirl. 80% Color, 11/16" d. Reverse of Figure 9-60.

Figure 9-64. Indian Swirl. 360° Color, 15/16" d. *Collection of Jerry Biern.*

Figure 9-65. Indian Swirl. 360° Color, 15/16" d. End view of Figure 9-64. *Collection of Jerry Biern.*

Figure 9-69. Indian Swirl. Single Pontil, 11/16" d.

Figure 9-66. Indian Swirl. 360° Color, 21/32" d.

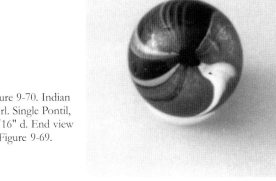

Figure 9-70. Indian Swirl. Single Pontil, 11/16" d. End view of Figure 9-69.

Figure 9-67. Indian Swirl. 360° Color, 21/32" d. End view of Figure 9-66.

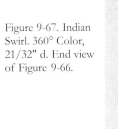

Figure 9-71. Indian Swirl. Maglite, blue glass, 360° color, 13/16" d.

Figure 9-68. Indian Swirl. Single Pontil, 15/16" d. *Collection of Jerry Biern.*

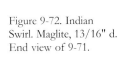

Figure 9-72. Indian Swirl. Maglite, 13/16" d. End view of 9-71.

Figure 9-73. Indian Swirl. Maglite, olive green glass, rare size, 1-5/8" d. *Collection of Jerry Biern.*

Figure 9-76. Indian Swirl. Maglite, purple glass, rare size, 1-5/8" d. *Collection of Jerry Biern.*

Figure 9-74. Indian Swirl. Maglite, 1-5/8" d. End view of Figure 9-73. *Collection of Jerry Biern.*

Figure 9-77. Indian Swirl. Maglite, blue glass, 360° color, 11/16" d.

Figure 9-75. Indian Swirl. Maglite, gray glass, rare size, 1-11/16" d. *Collection of Jerry Biern.*

Figure 9-78. Indian Swirl. Maglite, 11/16" d. End view of Figure 9-77.

Figure 9-81. Indian Swirl. Transparent, rare size, 1-3/4" d.

Figure 9-79. Indian Swirl. Transparent, blue glass, 21/32" d.

Figure 9-82. Indian Swirl. Transparent, 1-3/4" d. End view of Figure 9-81.

Figure 9-80. Indian Swirl. Transparent, 21/32" d. End view of Figure 9-79.

Figure 9-83. Indian Swirl. Clear glass, rare size, 2" d.

Figure 9-86. Indian Swirl. Transparent, 2" d. End view of Figure 9-85.

Figure 9-84. Indian Swirl. Clear glass, 2" d. End view of Figure 9-83.

Figure 9-87. Indian Swirl. Transparent, blue glass, rare size, 2" d. *Collection of Jerry Biern.*

Figure 9-85. Indian Swirl. Transparent, blue glass, rare size, 2" d.

Figure 9-91. Indian Swirl. Transparent, purple glass, ¾' d.

Figure 9-88. Indian Swirl. Transparent, 2" d. End view of Figure 9-87. *Collection of Jerry Biern.*

Figure 9-92. Indian Swirl. Transparent, purple glass, 21/32" d.

Figure 9-89. Indian Swirl. Translucent, blue glass, Submarine type, rare size, 2" d. *Collection of Jerry Biern.*

Figure 9-93. Indian Swirl. Transparent, 21/32" d. End view of Figure 9-92.

Figure 9-90. Indian Swirl. Translucent, 2" d. End view of Figure 9-89. *Collection of Jerry Biern.*

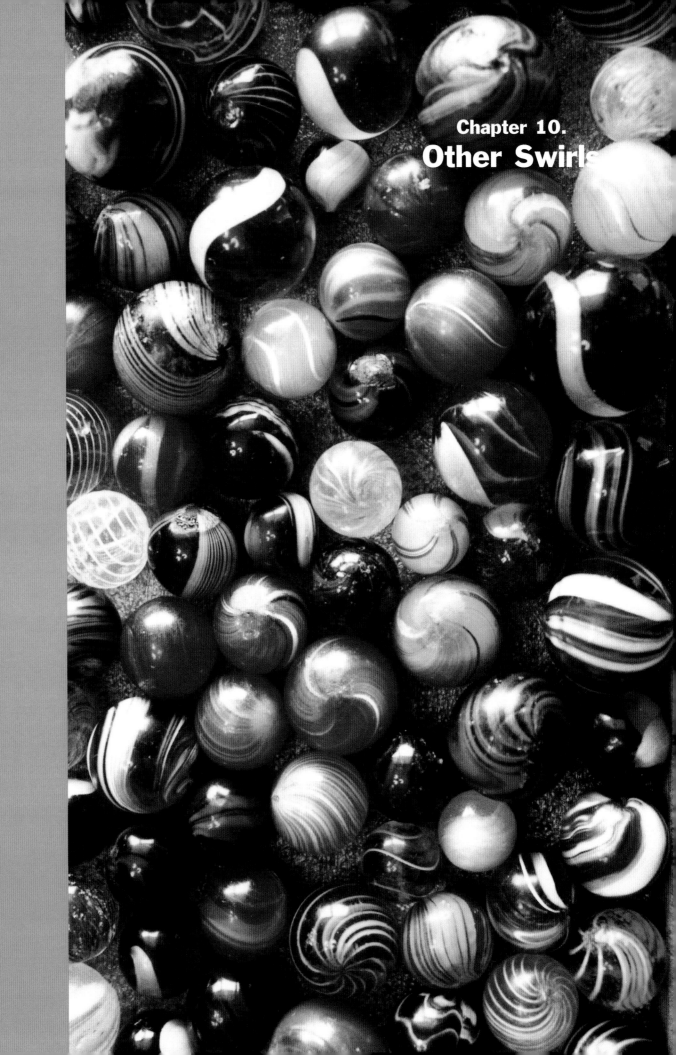

Chapter 10.
Other Swirls

Butterscotch and Custard Swirls

These terms refer to the base colors of these marbles. Custard is a translucent yellowish glass that contains some uranium trioxide, causing these marbles to fluoresce vividly under a black light. See Figures 10-28 through 10-36.

Caramel Swirls

These marbles have a base color of caramel candy. They may be semi-opaque or translucent brown. The shades of color may vary, but are usually a darker brown. See Figures 10-1 through 10-22.

Cornhusk Swirls

Cornhusk swirls are clear or colored transparent glass marbles with one wide band of white or yellow running near the surface from one pole to the other. See Figures 10-23 through 10-27.

English Style

These are brightly colored, well-designed marbles where the design is close to the surface of the marble. English style refers to both swirls and end-of-day marbles with vivid colors of red, yellow, orange, green, and blue. See Figures 10-37 through 10-50.

Gooseberry Swirls

The Gooseberry swirl is a transparent glass marble with uniform strands of glass all around and close to the surface of the marble. See Figures 10-51 through 10-72.

Mist Swirls

Marbles with a banded swirl design where there are many strands of translucent color on the surface design of the marble. See Figures 10-85 through 10-90.

Slag Glass Swirls

Slag Glass Swirls are glass marbles with patterns and colors that imitate marble, the mineral. Base colors usually are red, brown, green, blue, or purple with white mixed in each marble. See Figures 10-13 through 10-20, 10-73 through 10-84.

Miscellaneous Swirls

Size	Mint	Near-Mint	Good	Collectible
1/2" to 11/16"	80.00	50.00	25.00	15.00
3/4" to 1"	150.00	75.00	40.00	15.00
1-1/8" to 1-1/2"	Too rare to value			

*All values are in dollars. Above prices are representative for Caramel, Custard, Butterscotch, Cornhusk, Clear glass, Gooseberry, Mist, and Slag glass swirls.

Premiums for:		Examples:
With mica	3 to 5x	10-5, 10-6
English-style	2 to 5x	10-37 through 10-50
Mist	2 to 5x	10-85 through 10-90
Blue-glass Cornhusk	3 to 10x	10-25 through 10-27
Colored glass Gooseberries (except normal brown colors)	3 to 10x	10-67 through 10-72

Deductions for:	
Buffed surface	10 to 20%
Off-center or missing designs	20 to 40%
Ground and polished surface	20%
Annealing or other fractures	25 to 50%

Figure 10-1. Caramel Swirl, 11/16" d.

Figure 10-5. Caramel Swirl, with Mica, 21/32" d.

Figure 10-2. Caramel Swirl, 11/16" d. End view of Figure 10-1.

Figure 10-6. Caramel Swirl, 21/32" d. End view of Figure 10-5.

Figure 10-3. Caramel Swirl, 7/8" d.

Figure 10-7. Caramel Swirl, 11/16" d.

Figure 10-4. Caramel Swirl, 7/8" d. End view of Figure 10-3.

Figure 10-8. Caramel Swirl, 11/16" d. End view of Figure 10-7.

Figure 10-9. Caramel Swirl, 15/16" d.

Figure 10-12. Caramel Swirl, 15/16" d. End view of Figure 10-11.

Figure 10-13. Caramel Swirl, ¾" d.

Figure 10-10. Caramel Swirl, 15/16" d. End view of Figure 10-9.

Figure 10-14. Caramel Swirl, ¾" d. End view of Figure 10-13.

Figure 10-11. Caramel Swirl, 15/16" d.

Figure 10-15. Caramel Swirl, 11/16" d.

Figure 10-16. Caramel Swirl, 11/16" d. End view of Figure 10-15.

Figure 10-17. Caramel Swirl, 21/32" d.

Figure 10-20. Caramel Swirl, 21/32" d. End view of Figure 10-19.

Figure 10-18. Caramel Swirl, 21/32" d. End view of Figure 10-17.

Figure 10-21. Caramel Swirl, 21/32" d.

Figure 10-19. Caramel Swirl, 21/32" d.

Figure 10-22. Caramel Swirl, 21/32" d. End view of Figure 10-21.

Figure 10-23. Cornhusk swirl, amber glass, 5/8" d.

Figure 10-27. Cornhusk swirl, blue glass, 21/32" d.

Figure 10-24. Cornhusk swirl, olive green glass, 5/8" d.

Figure 10-28. Custard Glass swirl, ¾" d.

Figure 10-25. Cornhusk swirl, blue glass, 23/32" d.

Figure 10-29. Custard Glass swirl, ¾" d. End view of Figure 10-28.

Figure 10-26. Cornhusk swirl, blue glass, 21/32" d.

Figure 10-30. Custard Glass swirl, 21/32" d.

Figure 10-31. Custard Glass swirl, 21/32" d. End view of Figure 10-30.

Figure 10-34. Custard Glass swirl, 11/16" d.

Figure 10-35. Custard Glass swirl, 11/16" d. End view of Figure 10-34.

Figure 10-32. Custard Glass swirl, 21/32" d.

Figure 10-36. Custard Glass swirl, 5/8" d. *Collection of Elliot Pincus.*

Figure 10-33. Custard Glass swirl, 21/32" d. End view of Figure 10-32.

Figure 10-37. English Style swirl, 13/16" d.

Figure 10-38. English Style swirl, 13/16" d. End view of Figure 10-37.

Figure 10-41. English Style swirl, 11/16" d.

Figure 10-39. English Style swirl, 13/16" d.

Figure 10-42. English Style swirl, 11/16" d. End view of Figure 10-41.

Figure 10-40. English Style swirl, 13/16" d. End view of Figure 10-39.

Figure 10-43. English Style swirl, 13/16" d.

Figure 10-44. English Style swirl, 13/16" d. End view of Figure 10-43.

Figure 10-47. English Style swirl, 9/16" d.

Figure 10-45. English Style swirl, 11/16" d.

Figure 10-48. English Style swirl, 9/16" d. End view of Figure 10-47.

Figure 10-46. English Style swirl, 11/16" d. End view of Figure 10-45.

Figure 10-49. English Style swirl, 13/16" d.

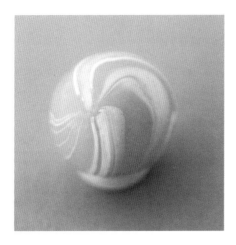

Figure 10-50. English Style swirl, 13/16" d. End view of Figure 10-49.

Figure 10-54. Gooseberry swirl, 13/16" d. End view of Figure 10-53

Figure 10-51. Gooseberry swirl, 15/16" d.

Figure 10-55. Gooseberry swirl, ¾" d.

Figure 10-52. Gooseberry swirl, 15/16" d. End view of Figure 10-51.

Figure 10-56. Gooseberry swirl, ¾" d. End view of Figure 10-55.

Figure 10-53. Gooseberry swirl, 13/16" d.

Figure 10-57. Gooseberry swirl, 11/16" d.

Figure 10-58. Gooseberry swirl, 11/16" d. End view of Figure 10-57.

Figure 10-62. Gooseberry swirl, 11/16" d. End view of Figure 10-61.

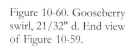

Figure 10-59. Gooseberry swirl, 21/32" d.

Figure 10-63. Gooseberry swirl, 11/16" d.

Figure 10-60. Gooseberry swirl, 21/32" d. End view of Figure 10-59.

Figure 10-64. Gooseberry swirl, 11/16" d. End view of Figure 10-63.

Figure 10-61. Gooseberry swirl, 11/16" d.

Figure 10-65. Gooseberry swirl, 9/16" d.

Figure 10-66. Gooseberry swirl, 9/16" d. End view of Figure 10-65.

Figure 10-70. Gooseberry swirl, 11/16" d. End view of Figure 10-69.

Figure 10-67. Gooseberry swirl, 13/16" d.

Figure 10-71. Gooseberry swirl, 13/16" d.

Figure 10-68. Gooseberry swirl, 13/16" d. End view of Figure 10-67.

Figure 10-72. Gooseberry swirl, 13/16" d. End view of Figure 10-71.

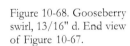

Figure 10-69. Gooseberry swirl, 11/16" d.

Figure 10-73. Slag Glass swirl, amber glass, 1" d.

Figure 10-74. Slag Glass swirl, 1" d. End view of Figure 10-73.

Figure 10-77. Slag Glass swirl, purple glass, 13/32" d.

Figure 10-80. Slag Glass swirl, 11/16" d. End view of Figure 10-79.

Figure 10-75. Slag Glass swirl, purple glass, 13/16" d.

Figure 10-78. Slag Glass swirl, 13/32" d. End view of Figure 10-77.

Figure 10-81. Slag Glass swirl, green glass, ¾" d.

Figure 10-76. Slag Glass swirl, 13/16" d. End view of Figure 10-75.

Figure 10-79. Slag Glass swirl, purple glass, 11/16" d.

Figure 10-82. Slag Glass swirl, ¾" d. End view of Figure 10-81.

Figure 10-83. Slag Glass swirl, green glass, 11/16" d.

Figure 10-87. Mist swirl, 13/16" d.

Figure 10-84. Slag Glass swirl, 11/16" d. End view of Figure 10-83.

Figure 10-88. Mist swirl, 13/16" d. End view of Figure 10-87.

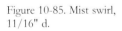

Figure 10-85. Mist swirl, 11/16" d.

Figure 10-89. Mist swirl, 13/16" d.

Figure 10-86. Mist swirl, 11/16" d. End view of Figure 10-85.

Figure 10-90. Mist swirl, 13/16" d. End view of Figure 10-89.

Glossary of Terms

ANNEAL. The process of gradually reducing glass temperatures, usually in an oven or lehr, for the purpose of balancing internal stresses throughout the glass, resulting in the prevention of fractures when the object reaches room temperature.

ANTIQUE. According to United States custom laws: an item, usually a work of art, furniture, or decorative object made at least one hundred years ago. In the hobby of marbles, those from World War I and earlier are considered "antique marbles."

AVENTURINE. Type of glass containing small articles of either copper (goldstone), chromium oxide (green aventurine), or ferric oxide (red aventurine) giving glass an intensely glittering appearance (*see* LUTZ).

BANDED. Stripes of contrasting color curving pole to pole on handmade marbles—either on, in, or very near the surface.

BATCH. A mixture of raw materials used to make glass.

BLOWN GLASS. A glass object that is formed using blown air, as opposed to rolling, drawing, fusing, molding, etc. Marbles are not blown glass.

BOTTLE GLASS. Glass made from natural materials, no coloring agents added. Usually green, blue, or amber tint.

BRUISED. The CONDITION of a marble that has received a visibly damaging blow, but no part has been chipped off. Sometimes this condition does not reduce the value quite as much as chips. *See also* CONDITION.

BUTTERSCOTCH SWIRL. Marbles with a base color appearance of butterscotch pudding. Such marbles may be opaque, semi-opaque, or translucent, and have a surface design of a different color.

CANDLE SWIRL. A type of handmade swirl marble with latticinio center, usually with an outer decoration of varying color bands running in a spiral from pole to pole. *See also* LATTICINIO.

CANDY SWIRL. A type of handmade swirl marble that has a center that looks similar to Christmas candy. *See also* SOLID CORE *and* LOBED CORE.

CANE. A glass rod from which handmade marbles are fashioned. The rod is typically constructed layer upon layer of clear and contrasting colors.

CARAMEL SWIRL. Marbles with a base color appearance of caramel, which may be semi-opaque or translucent brown. The shades of color may vary.

CASE GLASS. The glass covering on onionskins and swirls, usually CRYSTAL, but transparent colors over crystal body glass can occur (*see* CRYSTAL).

CHIPS. Pieces broken from the surface of a marble.

CLAMBROTH. A type of handmade glass marble. The body is one color, with evenly spaced, narrow color-strands running from pole to pole in the surface glass. May have sequences of two or more strand colors (also multicolored strands) occurring. The term CLAMBROTH is correctly reserved for this type when the body is milk glass (the color of clambroth).

CLEARS. A type of handmade glass marble. The body glass is transparent.

CLEARY. A type of machine made marble of undecorated transparent glass.

COFFIN BOX. Boxes used by the maker or distributor to sell sets of graduated sizes of a marble design. The name comes from the box shape being the same as coffins of that era.

COLLECTIBLE. The worst marble condition expected in a collection. Badly damaged, but has some redeeming features. *See also* CONDITION.

COLLECTOR. One who gathers specimens for the purpose of study or ornament. Contrasts with accumulator in implying more careful selection that leads to enjoyment of the aesthetic values pursued . . . and the knowledge gained and shared in fellowship.

COMPATIBILITY. The mutual characteristics of two or more batches of glass that allow them to be fused together, and after proper cooling retain no stresses which will result in fractures. *See also* ANNEAL *and* BATCH.

CONDITION and GRADING. The grading of condition is very subjective. Every collector has their own opinion and no two collectors will likely agree on the exact condition of a particular marble. The Marble Collectors Society of America uses a descriptive grading system (**Mint, Near Mint, Good, Collectible**), which allows for some flexibility in grading. A numerical grading system based on a scale of 1 to 10 has also developed among marble collectors. The descriptions of each grading label used by the Society, along with the equivalent numerical grading is:

Mint: A marble that is in original condition. The surface is unmarked and undamaged. There may be some rubbing on the surface; however, the marble is just the way it came from the factory. (10.0-9.0)

Near Mint: A marble that has experienced minor usage. There may be evidence of some hit marks, usually tiny subsurface moons, pinprick chips, tiny flakes, or tiny bruises. The damage is inconsequential and does not detract from viewing the marble. If there is noticeable damage, and it is on only one side of the marble the other side is considered Mint. (8.9-8.0)

Good: A marble that has experienced minor usage. It will have numerous hit marks, subsurface moons, chips, flakes, or bruises. The core can still be clearly seen, but the marble shows obvious use. If the damage is large or deep, and it is confined to one side the other side is considered Mint to Near Mint. (7.9-7.0)

Collectible: A marble that has experienced significant usage. Overall moons, chips, flakes, and bruises. The core is completely obscured in some spots. A collectible marble has served its purpose and been well used. Still, it is a placeholder in a collection until a better example replaces it. (6.9-6.0)

Any damage to the surface of a marble, no matter how slight, will affect its value. For a given amount of damage, the depreciation of value is much greater for machine made marbles than for handmade marbles. Even a small chip will effectively reduce the value of a machine made marble by more than half. Collectors tend to be more forgiving of damage to a handmade marble; this is likely because handmade marbles are more difficult to find.

The size of a marble is generally measured by its diameter in inches. Marble manufacturers utilize a sieve system of measuring. Using a device that measured marbles in 1/16 inch increments, the smallest opening that a marble would fall through was its size. Because of this method, the marbles classified as one size by a manufacturer could in fact vary by 3/64 inch. It is technically impossible to produce a handmade glass marble in sizes greater than approximately 2-1/2 inches in diameter because the marble would sag and deform during the annealing process due to its weight. However, different types of marbles are more common in some size than others. Machine made marbles are usually ½ inch to ¾ inch. This is because marble tournament regulations set the size of the shooters to be between ½ inch and ¾ inch and the size of the target marbles to be 5/8 inch. Again, the relative rarity of different sizes varies greatly from one type of marble to another.

CORNHUSK. Clear or colored transparent glass marbles with one wide opaque band of yellow or white running from pole to pole near the surface of the marble.

COTTAGE MARBLES. Machine made marbles not produced by a major manufacturer were produced by one of numerous cottage industries or "backyard glass shops" that were producing marbles during the 1920 and 1930s.

CROSSOVERS. Marbles that span two categories or have features of two categories. These can include errors or oddities, e.g., a divided core swirl where the core bands are placed so close together they form a solid or lobed solid core.

CRYSTAL. Clear, colorless glass, the body and case glass of most handmade marbles. Colorless as compared with colored transparent glass.

CUSTARD GLASS. Translucent yellow-green glass containing uranium trioxide as pigment which causes custard glass to be vividly florescent under black light. *See also* VASELINE GLASS.

CUTOFFS. The two rough spots on opposite poles of handmade marbles made from canes. Often mistakenly called "pontils," these rough spots show the marble was handmade (possibly in Germany before 1910). The presence of only one rough spot indicates that the marble may have been made from a gather on the end of a punty (pontil). The spot is then correctly called a pontil mark. Rough spots found (as they are occasionally) on machine made marbles indicate that some variable was out of adjustment in the manufacturing process (e.g., the glass may not have been hot enough to smooth out in the forming rollers). This is true even when referring to transition marbles that were hand-gathered on a pontil rod then machine-rounded on forming rollers. *See also* PONTIL *and* PUNTY.

DIAMETER. The length of a straight line through the center of an object. The size of a marble is measured by its greatest diameter.

DING. Minor damage to a marble caused by a blow, resulting in a small chip missing.

DIVIDED CORE SWIRL. Type of handmade SWIRL marble having a core of two or more varicolored ribbons from pole to pole. Transparent glass at the marble's center is visible. Normally having the same number of sets of outer strands or bands as the number of core bands. *See also* SOLID CORE, DOUBLE RIBBON, *and* SWIRL.

DOUBLE RIBBON. A variety of handmade ribbon core SWIRL having two ribbons, matching or contrasting, parallel to each other which extend from pole to pole. *See also* SOLID CORE, RIBBON CORE, *and* SWIRL.

END-OF-CANE. A rare handmade marble that is actually a craftsman's imperfect. It comes from so near the end of the cane (perhaps the first marble from that cane) that all of the intended colors were not included in the marble—usually an ugly marble. *See also* SWIRL.

END OF DAY. A class of marbles, usually with multiple colors. A term taken from other antique glassware using glass left at the end of the day.

ENGLISH SWIRL. Vibrant brightly colored marbles where the origin is close to the surface. Refers to both swirls and End-of-Day marbles with the vivid colors of red, yellow, orange, and green.

EXCELLENT. An obscure term when referring to the condition of a marble. Mint is less subjective, and has been recognized to best describe the best condition of a marble that remains undamaged but not in its original packaging. *See also* MINT *and* CONDITION.

FURNACE. Any of various ovens used for melting the glass batch. A kiln.

GATHER. A portion of molten glass on a pontil. *See also* METAL, PUNTY, *and* PONTIL.

GENERAL GRANT GAME. An early form of the board game "Solitaire." This game board was round and had a hand painted silhouette of the bust of Grant on the surface of the board.

GERMAN SWIRL. Handmade glass marbles made in Germany. Most were made before 1910.

GLASS. An amorphous (uncrystallized) substance consisting ordinarily of silica (as sand), an alkali (as potash or soda) and some other alkali (as lime or lead oxide) fused together. Various colors are imparted by the addition of metallic oxides. *See also* BATCH *and* METAL.

GLORY HOLE. An opening into the furnace or kiln. Used for reheating the gather of glass (the marble) when making a piece on a punty. *See also* PONTIL.

GOOD. Third from best CONDITION on a scale of four. *See also* CONDITION.

GOOSEBERRY. A transparent glass marble with uniform strands of glass close to the surface.

GRADING. See CONDITION.

GROUND. Refers to repairing a marble when considerable outer glass must be removed. If done by an expert, by hand, pontil marks may possibly be saved. When done on a sphere grinder, pontil marks are removed. When done in a rock tumbler the marble is usually ruined.

HANDMADE. Marbles made without use of machines, the exception being those held in the fingers against a power driven grinding wheel (e.g., agates made before 1910). Few handmade marbles of any sort can be expected to be perfect spheres; clay, pottery, and china types are most out-of-round.

INDIAN SWIRL. Handmade marble of dark base glass with colorful strands applied to the surface. Base glass may be opaque, semi-opaque, or translucent. Usually does not have a casing layer of glass.

KILN. Any various ovens, furnaces, used for the purpose of melting the glass batch, typically of brick construction, ceramic fiber lined, and in the larger sizes, heated with natural gas. *See also* LEHR *and* ANNEAL.

LATTICINIO. 1. Filigree glass of Venetian invention. Appears to have spiraling, crossing, or interlacing fine opaque threads in crystal base. 2. A type of handmade SWIRL marble with filigree center core.

LATTICINIO CORE. Innermost part of SWIRL made of latticinio glass (also called filigree, lace, or net core).

Marbles commonly have a colorful outer decoration spiraling from pole to pole. See also CANDLE SWIRL *and* SWIRL.

LEHR. An oven in which glassware is annealed, typically fitted with a continuous belt feed. *See also* ANNEAL *and* KILN.

LOBED. One of the types of cores in a marble. Occurs in SOLID CORE SWIRLS and END-OF-DAY marbles.

LOBED CORE. A type of SOLID CORE that has a cross-sectional shape of a cogwheel, cloverleaf, or other repeated pattern of flutes, ribs, vanes, or grooves. Solid cores show a crystal center when sawed in half. If the clear center is visible, the marble's value is reduced. Solid cores are not to be confused with Peltier catseye machine made marbles. *See also* CANDY SWIRL, SINGLE RIBBON, DIVIDED CORE, *and* SOLID CORE.

LUTZ. A handmade glass marble containing aventurine. This type occurs in most designs of SWIRLS. *See also* AVENTURINE. Named after the man, Nicholas Lutz, who first made this type of glass.

MARBLE SHEARS. The tool used to hold, form, and cut a handmade marble as it is being made from the hot cane. Similar to tongs or sheep shears, but having a cup on one side and a blade on the other.

MARBLES. Marbles are little balls made of hard substances (as stone, glass, porcelain, clay, metal, etc.) typically from 5/8 inch to 2 inches in diameter. Decorative marbles are as large as 3 inches and as small as $\frac{1}{4}$ inch.

METAL. Glass in its molten state is called metal.

MICA. 1. Mineral silicates that cleave into thin sheets—usually reflective, often silvery (most other colors occur). 2. A type of handmade glass marbles, a majority of which are Clears with flecks of mica interspersed within the marbles. Mica was introduced intentionally into some onionskins, and accidentally intruded into most other handmade marbles as craftsman's defects. *See also* CLEARS.

MINT. Established by long usage as the standard term meaning the original, undamaged condition. See also CONDITION.

MIST SWIRL. Swirls having many translucent colored strands as part of the surface design of a marble.

NEAR-MINT. Refers to condition of a marble. Accepted by usage as the next best grade after MINT. *See also* CONDITION.

OPAQUE. 1. Impervious to the rays of light, neither transparent nor translucent. 2. Type of handmade glass marble made of opaque glass that may be decorated with bands extending from pole to pole. The BANDED OPAQUE family, like the BANDED CLEAR family, has a more formal, controlled, precise, prim pattern of color arrangement than the brushed-on look of the INDIAN family. *See also* INDIAN SWIRL.

PEE WEE. Refers to a marble with $\frac{1}{2}$ inch or smaller maximum diameter.

PEPPERMINT SWIRL. A type of handmade glass marble. Easily identified because it looks like a ball of peppermint candy, usually red, white, and blue. Reportedly a United States centennial commemorative marble when it contains mica flakes in the blue banding. Construction is similar to an ONIONSKIN, with the inner design close to the surface.

POLE. Refers to the two opposite points on a handmade marble where the decorations terminate, and cut-off marks should be found. *See also* CUT-OFF *and* PUNTY.

POLISHING. Removal of haze from the surface of a marble. When done properly, polishing does not reduce the value of the marble, and can greatly increase its beauty. Performed in a way (similar to grinding) where the polishing compound is applied to a cotton buffer.

PONTIL. A long, steel rod. A device used to make the gather, to turn the gather while forming the marble, to finish and to fire polish. Also called a punty. *See also* PUNTY.

PONTIL MARK. A rough mark left on one or both poles of a handmade marble where the marble was sheared off the rod or the end of the punty. A cut-off mark left on the marble.

POOR. Refers to condition of a marble. Marble has serious damage, chips, and/or cloudy surface. *See also* CONDITION.

PUNTY. An iron or steel rod used to fashion hot glass that is attached by a rod of glass first gathered on the punty. Where detached from the glass, it leaves a rough spot.

RIBBON CORE. A rare type of handmade SWIRL having one flat ribbon that spirals through the center from pole to pole. *See also* SWIRL, SPIRAL, SINGLE RIBBON SWIRL, DOUBLE RIBBON, *and* DIVIDED CORE.

SEED BUBBLES. Tiny air bubbles in old glass. Deliberately placed seed bubbles in contemporary handmade marbles.

SEEDY GLASS. Glass containing many small gaseous inclusions (bubbles), usually introduced intentionally into the base glass of both handmade and machine made marbles to create visual texture. *See also* SWIRL MARBLES.

SINGLE PONTIL. Term for handmade marbles having only one cut-off mark, includes MICAS, SLAGS, and miscellaneous oddities.

SINGLE RIBBON. A variety of handmade SWIRLS with a flat ribbon shaped core, either thick or thin. *See also* RIBBON CORE *and* SOLID CORE.

SIZES. Marble size is usually measured with Vernier Calipers or circle templates. Generally, the sizes used for antique marbles are the diameters in sixteenths of an inch up to one inch and in eighths of an inch and above.

SLAG. Types of marbles made of slag glass, either handmade or machine made.

SLAG GLASS. 1. A glass pattern that simulates the mixture of hues found in natural variegated stone marble and agate. Slag glass may be transparent as well as opaque. A marbled glass blended without predetermined pattern—variegated. 2. The glasslike waste from metal smelting furnaces.

SOLID CORE. A type of handmade glass SWIRL marble having a center decoration that appears to be a solid geometric shape extending from pole to pole. The core is typically white, sometimes yellow, rarely other colors, and commonly decorated with colored strands or ribbons. Outer decorative lines of color are usually present near the marble's surface. See also CANDY SWIRL, RIBBON CORE SWIRL, *and* SPIRAL.

SOLITAIRE. Popular marble game of the nineteenth century. Played by one player using a round board (General Grant Board) incised with thirty-three round depressions. The object of the game is to remove each jumped marble (as in the game of checkers, draughts) so that one marble remains resting in the center spot on the board. *See also* GENERAL GRANT GAME BOARD.

SPIRAL. Winding, curving, coiling, or circling around a center or pole and more or less receding (or approaching) it. The path of the decorations of most swirls marbles. Term sometimes applied to a SWIRL. *See also* SWIRL.

STRIAE. Elongated wavy imperfections in glass. May be bubbles or caused by unequal density of glasses used. Striae causes variation in intensity of hues, as in stained glass windows.

SWIRL. 1. A whirling motion or something characterized by such a motion, whirl, curve, or twist around a point or line. 2. A type of HANDMADE glass marble with ribbons or strands of colored glass twisted around the inside axis. May have incidental mica chips or may contain bands with aventurine. The aventurine sometimes occurs in green or blue translucent bands. *See also* SPIRAL, LATTICINIO, SINGLE RIBBON, *and* SOLID CORE SWIRL.

WET MINT. Referring to CONDITION of a marble. Wet mint look can be applied to the surface of a marble with a coating of liquid acrylic floor wax. *See also* CONDITION, MINT, *and* POLISH.

Bibliography

Barrett, Marilyn. *Aggies, Immies, Shooters and Swirls: The Magical World of Marbles.* Little, Brown and Company, 1994.

Baumann, Paul. *Collecting Antique Marbles.* Wallace Homestead Book Co., 1991, 2000.

Bergstrom, Evangeline H. *Old Glass Paperweights.* New York: Crown Publishers, 1940.

Block, Robert. *Marbles: Identification and Price Guide.* Atglen, Pennsylvania: Schiffer Publishing, Ltd., 1996, 1998.

Block, Stanley. *Marble Mania.* Atglen, Pennsylvania: Schiffer Publishing, Ltd., 1998.

Block, Stanley. "Marbles—Playing for Fun and For Keeps." *The Encyclopedia of Collectibles—Lalique to Marbles.* Time-Life Publications, 1983.

Chestney, Linda. "Collectibles: Marbles." *New Hampshire Profiles,* April 1984: 29-32, 37, 48-49 (30, 48).

Garland, Robert. "That 's Marbles, Son." *Saturday Evening Post,* 13 July 1946: 69.

Grist, Everett. *Antique and Collectible Marbles.* Paducah, Kentucky: Collector Books, 1992.

Grist, Everett. *Big Book of Marbles.* Paducah, Kentucky: Collector Books, 1993.

Howe, Bea. "The Charm of Old Marbles." *Country Life,* 11 December 1969: 1593.

Huffer, Lloyd and Chris Huffer. "Marbles: Today 's Game is Collecting." *Antiques And The Arts Weekly,* 11 May 1990: 1, 108-110.

Ingram, Clara. *The Collector's Encyclopedia of Antique Marbles.* Paducah, Kentucky: Collectors Books, 1972.

Johnson, Owen. "In Marble Time: The Ruling Passion of Boys, Small and Large, Near and Far, When the Warm Days of Springtime Come." *Colliers,* 15 April 1911: 23, 42.

Lidz, Franz. "Spotlight: Here 's a Man Who Has All of His Marbles—Maybe Some of Yours, Too." *Sports Illustrated,* 3 December 1984: 7.

Louis, Sally B. "Playing for Keeps: Collecting Antique Marbles." *New York-Pennsylvania Collector,* December 1985: 1B-2B, 4B.

"Marbles." *New York Time Magazine,* 20 July 1914: 2.

"Marbles." *Saturday Review,* 26 July 1884: 107-108.

McClinton, Katherine Morrison. "Marbles." *Antiques of American Childhood.* New York: Barmahall, 1970: 207-209.

Metzerott, Mary. "Notes on Marble History." *Hobbies,* November 1941: 56-57.

Randall, Mark E. and Dennis Webb. *Greenberg 's Guide to Marbles.* Sykeville, Maryland: Greenberg Publishing Co., 1988.

Smith, Linda Jean. "Lost Marbles." *Country Home Magazine,* April 1991.

Soble, Ronald L. "Your Collectibles: Losing His Marbles to Highest Bidder." *Los Angeles Times,* 20 March 1986, sec. 5: 20.

Watson, Henry D. "Antique Marbles of Stone, Pottery, and Glass. " *American Collector,* July 1942: 6, 7, 15.

Webb, Dennis. *Greenberg 's Guide to Marbles.* Second Edition. Sykeville, Maryland: Greenberg Publishing Co., 1994.

Appendices

Appendix I: Marbles on Computer

By now, most have found themselves bombarded with today's technology revolution—news of the Internet, World Wide Web, cyberspace, the Information Superhighway, "going on-line," and "net surfing." Marble collecting, and antiquing in general, using the Internet and on-line services is growing at a rapid pace. The Internet has provided collectors with a remarkably efficient means of communicating and exchanging information, as well as other previously non-traditional forms of buying and selling. There are a number of ways you can enhance your marble collecting experience by going "on-line."

Discussion Groups

By having conversations through computers with other collectors, you have another avenue to get your questions answered, buy and sell marbles, and find out about shows and auctions, using one of the on-line service "message boards." You can also participate in the Marble Collectors Mailing List and bulletin board at www.marblecollecting.com. There are also small groups on various networks and servers.

The World Wide Web

The World Wide Web is the fastest growing area for on-line collecting. There is a tremendous wealth of information on the "Web," and more is being added each day. The largest and most comprehensive marble related web site is marblecollecting.com. This site links to the MCSA's web site at www.marblemania.com; on-line version of the book *Marbles: Identification and Price Guide*; marble game instructions; marble show schedules; listing of marble clubs; auction information and links; Reproduction Alert page; and classified ads. Collectors are creating more marble related web sites seemingly every day. Marblecollecting.com has an up-to-date listing and links to numerous other marble web sites.

Auctions

Aside from buying and selling marbles on the Web through sites like eBay and Yahoo, you can also use the Internet to participate in marble auctions. Block's Box (www.blocksite.com) and Running Rabbit (www.runningrabbit.com) both list their catalogs with images on the Internet and accept valid bids via e-mail for their absentee auctions. Live CyberAuctions are also being held on-line today. A Chip Off The Old Block (www.blocksite.com) runs such live marble auctions twice weekly on the Internet.

So, whether you want to connect with other marble collectors, locate information on marbles and marble collectors, or buy and sell marbles, "cyberspace" has fast become an essential element in your collecting repertoire.

Appendix II: Marble Clubs

Following is a current listing of marble clubs.

Akro Agate Collector's Club
Roger Hardy
10 Bailey Street
Clarksburg, WV 26301

Badger Marble Club
Jim Stephenson
P.O. Box 194
Waunakee, WI 53597
Show

Blue Ridge Marble Club
Roger Dowdy
2401 Brookmont Court
Richmond, VA 23233
Show, newsletter

Buckeye Marble Collectors
Brenda Longbrake
P.O. Box 3051
Elida, OH 45807
Shows, newsletter

Canadian Marble Collectors Association
59 Mill Street
Milton, Ontario, Canada L9T JR8
Newsletters

Great Plains Marble Club
c/o Steve Campbell
508 Sixth Street
Glenwood, IA 51534
Show

Indiana Marble Club
Beth Morris
4803 Ridge Road
Kokomo, IN 46901
765-457-2477
Show

Knuckledown Marble Club
Daniel Ambrose
3112 Amherst Road
Erie, PA 16506

Maine Marble Club
Micki Pasanen
47 Burnham Road
Gorham, ME 04038
Show

Marble Collectors Society of America
Stanley Block
P.O. Box 222
Trumbull, CT 06611
Newsletter, books, videos, other publications

Marble Collectors Unlimited
Beverly Brule
P.O. Box 201
Northboro, MA 05132
Show, newsletter

Midwest Marble Club
Kenneth Royer, treasurer
3 Mallard Lane
St. Paul, MN 55127
Show, newsletter

Oklahoma Marble Collectors
c/o Neil or Debbie Thacker
16328 South Peoria
Bixby, OK 74008
Shows

Sea-Tac Marble Club
Larry Van Dyke
P.O. Box 336111
North Las Vegas, NV 89031
Shows, newsletter

South Jersey Marble Collectors
Joseph C. Brauner Jr.
7709 Raymond Drive
Millville, NJ 08322

Southern California Marble Collectors Society
Sherry Ellis
P.O. Box 6913
San Pedro, CA 90734
Show

Sun Coast Marble Collectors Society
Catherine Kortvely
P.O. Box 60213
St. Petersburg, FL 22784
Show, newsletter

Texas Marble Collectors
John W. Tays
417 Marsh Oval
New Braunfels, TX 78130
Shows, meeting

Tri-State Marble Collectors Club
David French
P.O. Box 18924
Fairfield, OH 45018
Show

Appendix III: Marble Shows

Shows and the dates they are held change each year. Listed below are the shows that were scheduled in 2001. It is best to call the show coordinators shown to verify future dates and locations.

January
Shawnee Marble Show
Ullin, IL
Steven Johnson 618-833-3399
Santa Cruz Marble Festival
Holiday Inn
Santa Cruz, CA
Larry Van Dyke 702-656-1513

February
Buckeye Marble Collectors Club Winter Show and Sale
Holiday Inn
New Philadelphia, OH
Steve Smith 330-364-8658.
Suncoast Marble Collectors Annual Winter Show
Best Western Mirage
St. Petersburg, FL 33714
Catherine Kortvely 727-528-0699
Susan Tokarz 727-535-7870.

March
Ozark Marble Show
Springdale, AR
Taunya Kopke 501-582-0882

Baltimore Washington Marble Show
Perry Hall Middle School
Perry Hall, MD
Joan Hayden 410-893-4929
Sea-Tac Marble Collectors Show
Holiday Inn - Sea-Tac
Seattle, WA 98188
Larry Van Dyke 702-656-1513

April
Illinois Meet
Super 8 Motel
Ottawa, IL
Gino or Randy Biffany 815-434-4391
Pride of the Prairie Marble Meet
Room hopping only - no show
Country Inn and Suites
Decatur, IL
Guy Gregg 217-795-4845
Texas Marble Collectors
Red Roof Inn
Garland, TX
Ron Roberts 214-352-8034

Northboro Marble Show
American Legion Hall
Northboro, MA
Carl Popp 508-842-7098
Beverly Brule 508-393-2923

May
West Virginia Marble Festival
WV Museum of American Glass
Cairo, WV
Dean Six 304-643-2217
Maine Marble Meet
Governor's Restaurant
S. Portland, ME 04106
Mickie Pasanen 207-839-4726
Marble Show
Holiday Inn
Wytheville, VA
Junior Stoots, 540-236-2249

June
Marble Collectors Unlimited
Holiday Inn, Amana Colonies
Amana Colonies, IA
Gary Huxford 319-642-3891

July

Marble Collectors Show
Holiday Inn - Tulsa South
Broken Arrow OK
Neil or Debbie Thacker 918-322-9221
Texas Marble Collectors
Holiday Inn
Victoria, TX 77901
Jerry Thompson 361-785-4303
Badger Marble Club Show
Quality Inn South
Madison, WI
Bill Bass 608-723-6138

August

Golden Gate Marble Show
Comfort Inn
1390 El Camino Real
Millbrae, CA
Larry Van Dyke 702-656-1513
Buckeye Marble Collectors
Lenox Inn
Reynoldsburg, OH
Brenda Longbrake 419-642-5191
Great Plains Marble Meet
Holiday Inn
Council Bluffs IA
Steve Campbell 712-527-9162
Mile High Marble Show
Red Lion Inn – Central
Denver, CO
Larry Van Dyke 702-656-1513

September

Low Country Marble Show
N. Charleston, SC
Mickey or James Gifford 843-835-8409
Crossroads of American Marble Show
Johanning Convention Center
Kokomo, IN
Beth Morris 765-457-2477
Houston Marble Show
Woody Newman 281-493-0808
Mountain Home Marble Show
Ramada Inn
Mountain Home, AR
Ken Dunteman, 870-424-7274
Midwest Marble Club
Thunderbird Hotel
Bloomington, MN
Dorothy Vayder 612-831-3066
Sisterville Marble Show
Gaslight Theater
Sisterville, WV
Jim King 1-800-296-4030

October

Northeast Marble Meet
Radisson Inn
Marlborough, MA
Bert Cohen, 617-247-4754

Cincy Marble Show
Holiday Inn North
Cincinnati, OH
Cliff Himmler 513-232-4223
Texas Marble Collectors Show
Holiday Inn
New Braunfels, TX
John Tays 830-620-0217
Smoky Hill Marble Show
Red Coach Inn Convention Center
Salina, KS
Larry Sawyer 785-472-3256

November

The Fall MarbleFest Auction and Show
Holiday Inn Select
Stamford, CT
Robert Block 203-926-8448
Mark Block 203-268-1577
Las Vegas Show
Holiday Inn
Las Vegas, NV
Larry Van Dyke 702-656-1513

December

Tom & Huck Marble Show
Hannibal Inn
Hannibal, MO
John Hamon Miller 573-221-3900
Jack Noonan 573-588-7833

Marble Mania®. Stanley Block in cooperation with The Marble Collectors Society of America. The hobby of marble collecting is still in its infancy, with plenty of room for growth in all areas and for new collectors. Marble Mania is the definitive photographic guide to collecting. This book incorporates over 1,300 color photographs, as well as an in-depth text covering the main areas of interest and information on marble manufacturers. Here are marbles made of stone, minerals, and materials other than glass; early handmade, machine-made, and contemporary handmade glass marbles; games, toys, and other uses for marbles. A glossary of terms; bibliography; lists of clubs, societies, marbles shows; and a list of museums with marble collections are included as well as a list of winners of the U. S. National Marble Tournaments since their inception. A value guide is included for each marble shown.

Size: 8 1/2" x 11"   1,318 color photos   192pp.
Price Guide/Index
ISBN: 0-7643-0014-8   hard cover $34.95

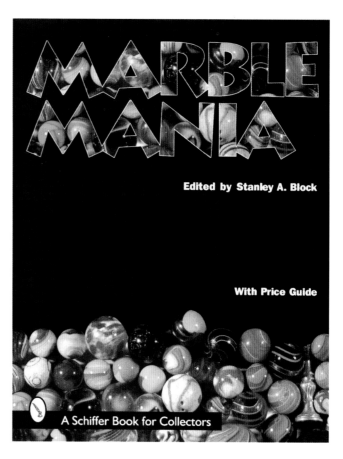

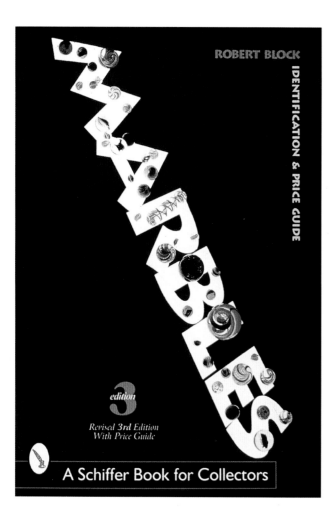

Marbles: Identification and Price Guide Revised 3rd Edition. Robert Block. Revised and expanded, here again is the fascinating world of marbles. Indians, Aggies, Steelies, and more...every major category of marble is presented in this new and exciting guide. Included are old handmade marbles of glass, earthenware, minerals, and steel; machine-made marbles and their manufacturers; and contemporary handmade glass marbles by artisans recapturing the old styles and creating exciting new styles all their own. Marble pricing is explained in detail. The author describes the four factors to look for when determining the value of a marble, and presents an accurate guide to today's market.

Size:6" x 9"   475 color photos   176pp
Price Guide
ISBN: 0-7643-0888-2   soft cover $19.95

Marbles Illustrated: Prices at Auction. Robert Block. This book provides a comprehensive guide to the actual selling prices of marbles during the past year. Utilizing a database of prices realized from over 6,000 marbles at auction during the past year, the author provides catalogue descriptions, pictures and values. Listings are categorized by marble type, allowing for easy reference for the collector.

Size: 6" x 9"   over 1500 marbles   160pp.
Price Guide
ISBN: 0-7643-0970-6   soft cover $16.95

Contemporary Marbles & Related Art Glass. Mark P. Block. Exquisite marbles produced by more than 130 artists and craftsmen are represented in over 600 stunning color photographs. The thorough text includes an extensive and detailed look at the pioneers, current artists, and craftsmen of the contemporary handmade marble movement. The history and development of handmade marbles is reviewed in words and illustrations, beginning with the earliest use of decorative glass and moving forward to the influence studio glass founders brought to bear on the pioneers and current craftsmen of contemporary handmade marbles. Also included are tips for the purchase and care of fine marbles, an in-depth glossary, and a valuation guide. This book will be a joy for everyone fascinated with glass. Novice and experienced art glass and marble collectors alike will appreciate this beautiful book.

Size: 9" x 12"   845 color photos   256pp.
Price Guide
ISBN: 0-7643-1166-2   hard cover $59.95

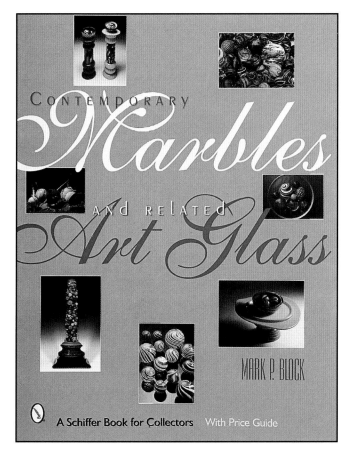